HAUNTED CAPE COD
The ISLANDS

HAUNTED CAPE COD
The ISLANDS

MARK JASPER

On Cape Publications

Yarmouth Port, Massachusetts

For additional copies or more information, please contact:

On Cape Publications,
P.O. Box 218,
Yarmouth Port, MA 02675, USA.
Or call toll Free: 1-877-662-5839.
e-mail: haunted@oncapepublications.com

First edition.

10   9   8   7   6   5   4   3   2   1

Printed in Canada.

Cover design by Debbie McLaughlin.

Layout and typography by DMAC dmac@mts.net.

Cover art by Karyn Frances Gray of
Damsel Fly Studio & Gallery
412 Route 6A, East Sandwich, MA 02537
508-888-7437
kfgartist@aol.com
www.thehudsons.com/karyngray.html

For Sharon and Hannah.

ACKNOWLEDGEMENTS

First and foremost, I would like to thank my wife, Sharon, for all of the help and support she has given me over the years. I would also like to thank the following organizations and people who helped make *Haunted Cape Cod & the Islands* become a reality: Sturgis Library, Chatham Historical Society, Mary Sicchio of Cape Cod Community College, Barbara Gill of the Sandwich Archives, Historian James Gould, Author Jack Sheedy, Attorney Doug Cabral, my publisher, Adam Gamble, and my copy editor, Stuard Derrick.

Table of Ghostly Contents

The Mid-Cape

INTRODUCTION

Who goes there? What foolish person would dare open a book like this? Do you have the slightest inkling about the mysterious world that you are edging towards? Well, do you? I thought not. It's not too late; you may still turn back if you wish. No one will accuse you of being cowardly. But for those hardy souls who dare to venture further, I will make a promise to you. At no time during your unearthly journey will I abandon you. If you happen to find yourself ambling down a dark, narrow hallway or creeping up a crooked, creaky staircase, be assured I will be beside you. If you veer off and find yourself trapped in a room shrouded in darkness and fear, don't panic.

If you will, think of the cover of this book as an ancient door. Just on the other side of that door you will meet many fascinating people. Some are alive, but most are not. Together we will explore the farthest reaches of Cape Cod and discover a world that has remained hidden for centuries... until now.

SOME QUESTIONS

Why write a book about haunted Cape Cod and the Islands? Why not write about lighthouses, cooking or the seashore? Cape Codders are hesitant to discuss otherworldly matters, so why pry into things that are better left untouched?

I will admit, researching ghostly activity on Cape Cod and the Islands was not an easy task. My former book, *Haunted Inns of New England,* took me a bit longer to write, because of the traveling that was involved; but at least there was no risk of running out of material. If one state began to dry up, I knew I had five more to go. But this is not the case for this narrow spit of land and offshore islands: Go too far in one direction and you're out in the ocean.

These lands are constantly changing and eroding. Researching the paranormal in such an abnormal location – a set of shifting sandbars in the sea – is no simple task. Prying spirited tales from the tongues of native Cape Codders is almost as difficult as trying to convince your two-year-old it's time to give up her Gummy Bear ice cream cone. Don't believe me? Then ask yourself why there has been so very little published on the subject in a region with more than four centuries of written history. Apology accepted.

Before we begin our journey, I will attempt to answer a few of the questions I am most frequently asked:

Q. How do you approach someone who lives in a haunted house?

A. My approach is usually quite simple and direct, but the response from the homeowner can vary greatly. If I'm having a good day, the conversation may go something like this:

Author: *"Good morning, madam. I was told that your house harbors a spirit or two. Any truth to the rumor?"*
Homeowner: *"Oh my, yes. We have all kinds of unusual happenings here. We even know the name of the ghost."*

Author: *"When would be a good time to get together?"*
Homeowner: *"We're around quite a bit. Just give me a call a few days in advance, and we'll be happy to meet with you."*
But if I'm having a bad day, the conversation might go something like this:

Author: *"Good evening, sir. Any truth to the rumor that your house might be haunted?"*
Homeowner: *"What did you say? I didn't hear you."*

Author: *"Is there any truth to the rumor that your house is haunted?"*
Homeowner: *"Is my house haunted? Is that what you asked?"*

Author: *"Yes."*
Homeowner: *"Is this some kind of joke?"*

Homeowner's wife: *"Who's on the phone?"*
Homeowner: *"Some nut asking me if our house is haunted. All right friend, who gave you our name?"*

Author: *"Sir, it's just a rumor I heard. If your house isn't haunted, I'll just move on."*
Homeowner: *"That's it, I'm calling the police."*

Q. Do you ever have trouble sleeping after hearing a frightening story?
A. If I ever get a good night's sleep after hearing a creepy story, I know it's time to stop writing about ghosts. I can think of nothing more enjoyable than a chilling tale that seeps into the marrow of your bones, causing one eye to remain open as your mind has its way with you.

Q. Do you believe in ghosts?
A. I often tell people who ask this question that I am simply a reporter and my opinions are not really pertinent. On the other hand, I will not duck the question. I don't believe the human race will be around long enough to decipher the mysteries of this vast universe. We know so little, yet we're quick to render an opinion one way or another. If a spirit world exists, then it exists. If it does not, then it does not. I did not write this book with the intention of proving or disproving anything. I wrote it because the subject truly fascinates me, and I have an insatiable appetite for the unknown. If you're looking for a direct response to the question, "Do you believe in ghosts?" then I am sorry I cannot give you a definitive answer, for I do not know nor do I want to. Simply put, the fun is in *not* knowing. That being said, my intuition tells me that something that cannot be explained away is happening in these old houses. I will leave it at that.

The
UPPER
CAPE

The White Paper Report

DILLINGHAM HOUSE BED & BREAKFAST

"**Yes**, we definitely have a ghost!" declared Ryan Griffin, owner of the beautifully restored Dillingham House Bed and Breakfast.

The Dillinghams for whom the house is named are noted as being one of the earliest European settlers on Cape Cod. Edward Dillingham was born in 1595 and died in 1667. He was one of the famous "Ten Men from Saugus" who founded Sandwich in 1637. A former Sandwich historian, Mr. George E. Burbank, believed the house was built in 1650; but historian Russell Lovell disagrees, believing the home was built in the Sagamore area by Simeon Dillingham, great grandson of Edward, in 1726 at the time of his marriage to Elizabeth Bourne. It is thought that Simeon's grandson,

Branch Dillingham, moved the house to its present location on Route 130 in Sandwich and raised it to a two-story dwelling around 1800. It has been noted that when Branch's first wife died, he remarried and had nine children. Branch Dillingham committed suicide in 1813.

The house was occupied by members of the Dillingham family until 1926, when it was purchased by Mr. Hardinge Scholle and his wife who used it as a summer home.

In 1938 the house was sold to Hannah M. Wescott who rented it to various people, including one tenant who operated it as a tavern and roadhouse. During the late thirties and early forties, the house began to be referred to sarcastically by local residents as "The Ritz," as the property gained a somewhat seedy reputation. Fistfights were not an uncommon occurrence.

The Dillingham House probably has one of the most haunted reputations on Cape Cod. Speculations about who these ghosts are have arisen but no one knows for certain. Some say it may be the ghost of Branch Dillingham, who committed suicide by drowning. Others insist the spirits are those of Branch's nine children who were orphaned after Branch's second wife died shortly after his own death. The children were rumored to have been left alone for long periods of time. Some have even claimed that if you knock on the walls at the Dillingham House, the children will sometimes knock back.

Ghostly apparitions have been known to appear here from time to time. One woman, while in one of the upstairs bedrooms, caught a glimpse of a stern looking man dressed in Victorian attire. And the woman's sister claims that when she awoke one morning, she found herself staring in disbelief at a little girl who was sitting at the end of her bed.

In the 1970s, the house remained vacant at various times. During this period local residents and neighbors reported seeing strange lights moving throughout the house. The police log verified that many years around Halloween the alarm in the house would sound for no apparent reason. During a routine check, one police officer reported seeing a rocking chair through the window gently rocking by itself.

Having heard the rumors of the Dillingham House hauntings some years ago, I tired with great persistence to interview one of the previous owners but was absolutely stonewalled. Fortunately for me, when Ryan Griffin became the new owner, she was willing to speak candidly. When Ryan first purchased the house, a friend dropped by for a visit with her dog, a beagle. As they relaxed at the kitchen table sipping wine, her friend's beagle began to investigate the house. When the dog found her way to the back staircase, she looked up the stairs and immediately began shaking and whimpering while backing away. This was the first sign of ghostly energy that Ryan took note of.

During renovations strong cooking odors began emanating from the living room where the original hearth and beehive oven are located. Ryan said the odors were gamy, like meat being fried. Other odors seemed to come from one of the guestrooms that was formerly a barroom back in the 1930s; just outside the door, her husband, Gert, was overcome by a strong blast of what he described as alcohol breath.

Some of her recent guests have heard eerie footsteps when no living person was around. And one guest, upon coming down for breakfast one morning, told Ryan that children kept seeping strangely into his dreams all night.

With all of these spirits lurking about, you might expect this sort of thing to unsettle an innkeeper who is new to the business. But Ryan isn't bothered a bit. She says the house flows with positive energy and she is always comfortable, even when it is otherwise empty. After all, you're never really alone in the Dillingham House!

I have included the following written report that I uncovered in the Sandwich Archives. It was written by a Sandwich police officer, James Foley, in 1979:

The Ghost House

Due to the increase of suspicious things that have been happening at the Dillingham House on Main St., this white paper report has been done. For those of you that do not know it, this particular house is presently lived in but is usually vacant by the owners during the week. It has been reported that a particular spirit inhabits the place.

It is hoped that this white paper report will put these suspicions to rest. The following is a list of the things that will help dispel these "rumors."

First of all, the house has a perimeter alarm and a motion detector alarm installed by Associated Alarms. As of late the motion detector has been activated by unknown factors in the house. The perimeter alarm has remained intact. On one occasion the motion detector was turned off and it still rang. Mysterious lights have been reported in the upstairs bedrooms described as flashlights. Upon arrival of the cruisers, the house has been in darkness. The alarm company has readjusted the alarm to minimum and still something inside the house has activated it. Within the last couple of days, the alarm company and one of our officers, after unlocking the back door, couldn't open it for a few minutes. A little later it opened with little effort. Last night one of our officers found the back door unlocked. The alarm did not activate. This officer then turned on the kitchen light and tired to turn on lights in the rest of the house, but failed. When he exited the house to get his flashlight, he returned to find that someone, or something, had turned the kitchen light off and turned the one in the living room on. Since this is the last reported case of mysterious happenings, we feel that there is no truth to the rumor that the house is haunted. Some of the things can be explained, but as of this writing, we have not been able to find anyone to explain them.

It has been noted that over the years there has been increased activity at the house during the month of October particularly when it gets close to All Soul's Day or commonly called Halloween. It is highly recommended that any officer entering this house act according to his or her feelings. In other words, if you feel like running, please do so. Screaming will also be allowed. It is requested however that upon exiting the house you at least slow down long enough to open the door and not go through it. Of course to cover all bases, a follow up report will follow this report with instructions as to what to do if you indeed encounter a spirit, spook, ghost or whatever. For now, rest easy.

DILLINGHAM HOUSE BED & BREAKFAST
SANDWICH, MASSACHUSETTS
508-833-0065

Just for Kicks

In the words of an anonymous man from Sandwich:

Well, essentially the house is a bow roof cape that was built either in 1718 or 1764. A woman who used to live here wrote a book about the house and describes it as being built in 1718. However, in the living room there is a brick in front of the fireplace that dates 1764, which I was told came out of the chimney when the chimney was being rebuilt back in the early 1950s.

As soon as I moved here, I began to have some interesting experiences. I was told by the author, who described the house as being haunted, that the last living descendent of the Hoxie family was a woman named Abigail Hoxie, who lived here until the beginning of the twentieth century. The author said she knew her when she was a child. She went on to say that Abigail didn't like visitors, especially visitors who didn't enjoy her flower gardens.

I have noticed that things over the years have become more harmonious around here since I started planting more flowers.

Before I owned the house, I was the caretaker here for another family. In the beginning, there was a little bit of violence involved whenever I stayed here alone. In the downstairs bedroom, there is a big four-poster bed. On more than one occasion, I awoke in the middle of the night feeling as if I was being kicked. One night I was being kicked so violently that I fled the house during a rainstorm and headed to my home in Boston. I was absolutely terrified. It felt like a boot of a man kicking me as hard as he could. I sat bolt upright in bed and it was terribly painful.

The night I left the house and headed for Boston, I was positive that some ghostly presence was in the car with me. When I was driving over the Sagamore Bridge, it was as if the presence jumped out of the car and was gone for good. It was also the last time I was ever kicked in the middle of the night.

Other interesting things have happened in the house as well. While I was still caretaker, the family who owned the house had an old rat-tailed hinged cabinet in the kitchen. On the top two shelves was a bunch of old New York World's Fair glasses. Since I was still the caretaker and they weren't mine, I didn't do anything with them. Personally, I would have thrown them out; I thought they were ugly. One Sunday evening, I remember going out to the market and getting a big two-pound tin of coffee. I specifically remember leaving the coffee on the kitchen table unopened. When I awoke the next morning, the tin was open, there was no coffee in it, and the New York World's Fair glasses had been turned upside down and were full of coffee grounds. I don't know how anyone would have done it. There wasn't a single ground on the shelf. It's certainly not something I would have done in my sleep, and of course there was no one else in the house.

Well, I thought that was a wonderful incident, and I actually began to enjoy it. There was never any fear after that presence got out on the Sagamore Bridge.

Little things continue to happen. Candlesticks will migrate during the night from the living room and will be found in front of the fireplace in the kitchen. Cups will be moved from one part of the house to another. There was a candle chandelier in the living room with a large turn ball at the base that I installed during the early eighties. I was married at the time, but my wife was dying of cancer. After she died, that ball in the chandelier would drop out every six months. I learned not to put anything underneath it because it would severely damage whatever was there. Whether that has anything to do with anything or not, I don't know, but it was just one more little thing.

Now, what other things have happened here? Whoever visits with me, and I don't mean living guests, seems to have a habit of picking up car keys and jingling them across the space of the bedroom in the middle of the night. I remember a couple that once stayed here. In the middle of the night, they heard their suitcase unclick and open. Apparently they had left their car keys inside. Suddenly they heard their keys go jingling across the bedroom. Well, they got up and stayed up the rest of the night with the lights on. They were just so terrified.

Invariably, about once a week, if I wake up in the middle of the night thinking about something, I will oftentimes hear what I call a cat jumping off the bed in the bedroom above mine. It's just the sound one would expect to hear if a cat jumped off a bed and landed on all fours. Frequently, I also hear the footsteps of a person walking across the room. I'm not alone in this experience. Another person that stayed in that room had the experience of hearing the cat and the footsteps as well. Nothing ever comes of it. They don't come downstairs, they don't make any noises, they don't holler or scream.

Over the fireplace in the living room, you can see what one might describe as the handprint of an elderly arthritic person, dragging itself across the woodwork in a crazed fashion leaving deeply embedded marks. I was told it was the handprint of Abigail Hoxie.

The woman who wrote the book about this house visited with me a few years ago. She began to elaborate on how she wrote the book based upon her experiences when she used to live here. Included in those experiences was a story about the night she was walking up the living room stairs with a candle. At the time there was no electricity here. While she was walking up, someone blew out the candle and pushed her down the stairs, which she said was one of the most frightening experiences of her life. She thought she knew who it was that pushed her, describing an angry old man that had lived here once upon a time. However, she believes the resident ghost who haunts this house is Abigail Hoxie.

Old Mother

THE SANDWICH VILLAGE HERB SHOP

I could be mistaken, but I do believe I am the first person to have documented a haunted herb shop, at least on Cape Cod. The Sandwich Village Herb Shop, located on Route 6A, features one of the largest selections of bulk herbs on the Cape, as well as many other items from natural bath products and tea blends to jewelry and tarot cards. The shop also features psychic readings in the cozy back room.

Michelle Tompkins-Regan started the herb shop in 1998, and it didn't take her long to realize there was something very strange in the shop. She described it as a "presence" that would often make the hair on the back of her neck stand on end.

Her first year in business, Michelle took her one-year-old daughter to work with her, and set up a crib and television in the back room. But over time, it became increasingly difficult to watch her daughter and operate the growing business, so she decided to put her daughter in day care. Whatever the "presence" was at The Sandwich Village Herb Shop, it certainly did not approve of Michelle's daughter being in day care. Right after her daughter left, things really began to go haywire. The back room became engulfed with an angry, almost confrontational type of energy that seemed to be directed towards Michelle, and she really felt the presence wanted her daughter back.

One year during the holiday season, Michelle remembers being alone in the shop, making up products for a gift show. She was in the back room when she suddenly began to hear a noise that sounded like someone screaming or wailing. She became so overcome with fright that she immediately fled from the shop. Not long after, Michelle sent her husband down to the shop at night to get something she had forgotten. When her husband returned, he told her that he had walked towards the back of the shop without turning the lights on, when suddenly he was stopped in his tracks by what he described as very angry energy. He also told Michelle that he heard a piercing scream and that every hair on his body stood on end. Michelle said after that incident, they felt they needed to do something. A group of friends got together and performed a type of spirit cleansing, which did seem to help. The aggressive side of this presence finally mellowed, but was by no means gone.

One night after a tarot class, a woman approached Michelle and said, "Did you see the woman standing behind the person at the end of the row?" Michelle said she saw no one. The woman had seen an old woman standing with her hand on a chair, observing the class. She wore a long 19th century dress and had her hair up in a bun.

Michelle vividly remembers the day when a man walked into the shop and asked her if he could walk into the back room. This was an odd request, but not a problem. When he came back into the front of the store, he said to Michelle, "Do you know the back of the store is haunted?" He said the spirit is an old woman who once lived in town and used to be a schoolteacher. He went on to say that she never had any children and that her husband had passed away. He also mentioned that she cries for him every night. The man indicated that her presence is all around the surrounding marsh, but for some reason enjoys hanging around the shop.

During an herb class, a woman once pulled Michelle aside and said, "Do you see her?" "Who?", Michelle replied. "The old mother," said the woman. "That's what they used to call her, because she never had any children and she used to take care of everyone else's children." Michelle then asked if she was a schoolteacher. The woman said she didn't know; the only other bit of information the spirit had communicated to her was that her husband had died and that she enjoys watching the people in the classes.

According to Michelle, "Old Mother," as she is now referred to, is not the only entity to haunt the herb shop. Quite a few customers have commented on the little black cat that dashes around the shop.

Of course, there is no black cat in the neighborhood, or at least not one that is alive. Even Michelle has seen this furry little creature, but says it's unclear whether the black cat has any connection to Old Mother.

So, if you're in the neighborhood and running low on herbs, pay a visit to this "spirited" little shop. Give my best to Old Mother... and don't forget to pat the kitty.

THE SANDWICH VILLAGE HERB SHOP
SANDWICH, MASSACHUSETTS
508-833-1933

Mrs. Wade

WOOD DUCK INN

Just a few short miles from the Bourne Bridge, in the peaceful village of Cataumet, rests a circa 1848 home known as the Wood Duck Inn. The moment I walked through the front door my heart started palpitating and my blood pressure shot up. Not because I had a premonition of otherworldly forces at the inn. Quite the opposite; actually I sensed some very real things. "It's OK guys, it's OK," I heard innkeeper Phil Duddy mutter. I usually begin to perspire when I hear words like these, because I know what's just around the corner. Without delay, I was greeted by the inn's two mascots, male and female Tibetan mastiffs. The gargantuan male dog who must have weighed two-hundred pounds resembled a cross between a black bear and a male lion, and the female wasn't much less intimidating. That being said, these two magnificent beasts were as friendly and docile as they were huge. After a few sloppy, sopping wet licks, each of which covered my entire face, Phil escorted them to the back of the inn, where they're usually kept while the place is occupied.

Phil proceeded to tour me around, starting in the Great Room, which is heavily influenced by his wife Dawn Champagne's fondness for antiques. Next up was the cozy living room with its comfortable furnishings and enormous brick hearth. During my tour I discovered the inn also sits atop a bluff overlooking one of the most scenic, working cranberry bogs on the Cape.

Guests with fine tastes have difficulty deciding whether to stay in the popular Treetops Suite, the romantic Garden Suite or the cozy

Cottage Room. All are exquisitely appointed with private baths. On the other hand, room choice is not difficult for those desiring to meet the ghost of one of the inn's former inhabitants, Mrs. Wade.

Phil revealed that a friendly elderly woman named Mrs. Wade once lived in the house before it was transformed into an inn. She is supposed to have died in the room now known as the Garden Suite. Phil's wife, Dawn, was actually the first to sense a presence emanating from this suite. She would often get strange, queasy feelings, particularly when she was carrying something down the stairs away from the Garden Suite. She began to think a ghostly presence was involved. Not certain how to deal with the situation, Dawn consulted a woman at work who claimed to have had experience with spirits. The woman simply suggested that Dawn talk to the spirit and explain to her that they have moved in and are seeking a friendly coexistence. Phil said Dawn took the woman's advice and did just that. Ever since then, Dawn has felt comfortable in the Garden Suite, even when she is alone.

Other people have reported peculiar happenings as well. Phil recalls two guests from Pennsylvania who stayed in the Garden Suite and woke up in the middle of the night to the sound of someone playing the spoons. The noise was so loud that one of the guests got out of bed, left the bedroom and went to sleep in another part of the suite on a daybed. Two other couples reported hearing loud clanking and banging noises while also residing there.

Without question, the most memorable incident happened on the night of Phil and Dawn's September wedding. Phil went into some detail about that special day: "When Dawn and I got married last September, we closed the inn for the weekend. We had all of our relatives jammed in here. Dawn's brother and wife were staying in one part of the Garden Suite and Jeff, Dawn's other brother, was staying in the other part of the Suite where the daybed is located. When Jeff went to bed that night, he wanted to see the [outdoor wedding] tent because it was brightly lit by lamps resembling half moons and stars. Jeff turned the light off in his room and fell asleep looking at the tent. He awoke in the middle of the night, and was startled by a glowing apparition of a woman dressed in white. This female ghost turned the light on and sat on his daybed. Jeff, who was not prone to exaggeration by any means, related the story to me the next morning." After a short while, the ghost, who was supposed to be that of Mrs. Wade, vanished.

WOOD DUCK INN
CATAUMET, MASSACHUSETTS
508-564-6404

Creepy Footsteps

In the words of an an anonymous woman from Pocassset:

I don't know how old the house is, nor do I own it, but I have been renting it for about five years. When I first moved in there was a room that I slept in that really gave me the creeps. I really don't know why, but it was always cold and gave off really bad vibes. I didn't give it much thought, just chalked it up to a room I didn't want to be in. So, I moved out of that room and moved upstairs. Well, about three months later at about three a.m. I awoke to the sound of very loud footsteps in my living room. The floorboards were really creaking. My cat immediately woke up, his fur was standing on end and his tail was puffed out. He was definitely aware that something was going on. I thought it was possible that it was my ex-boyfriend that came in to get something. So, I walked downstairs to investigate, but no one was there. I thought to myself, "OK," and went back upstairs and went to bed.

About a month later, I began to hear more strange noises. This time it sounded like the kitchen was being torn apart. I heard what sounded like dishes and other things being thrown around the room. The first thing I thought was, "What is the cat doing now?" I turned around and found the cat right next to me. I thought to myself, "Oh God!" I walked downstairs and found absolutely nothing. Everything was in its place and nothing was broken.

Several weeks after that I began to hear heavy footsteps coming up the stairs that would just suddenly stop. By now I knew there was a ghost in the house, but I was okay about it.

I did have some other strange occurrences as well; for instance, during the summer I would come home from work and find my outside light on. Now, I know it wasn't me because I never turn the outside light on in the summer. It's light when I leave, and it's light when I get home.

A door leading to my bedroom would sometimes be locked, even if I was pretty certain I had left it unlocked. Although, if I thought I had locked the door, I would usually find it unlocked. One time a large picture that I had resting on the fireplace mantle came crashing to the ground. It didn't just fall over; it was as if someone had picked it up and thrown it.

When I got my other cats I remember how they would slowly turn their heads around the room as if they were watching something.

Another time while I was in the bathroom looking in the mirror, I remember feeling something brush up against my neck. I knew it was too high for a cat's tail to reach and when I looked around there was not a cat to be found.

After a while the footsteps coming up the stairs at night began to make me feel uneasy. One afternoon I said out loud, "Hey look, you're scaring me. This has got to stop!" After that, I never heard anything again.

Spooky Mansion

HIGHFIELD HALL

L ooking like something straight out of a Stephen King novel, historic Highfield Hall would make even the most seasoned paranormal investigator shudder. It is the quintessential haunted mansion.

On a cold, raw April day, I had the good fortune of touring this incredible house with its Executive Director, Susan Shephard. This once magnificent home, now vacant and owned by the town of Falmouth, had seen better days. I was informed that a multimillion-dollar restoration project was in the works, so that in time, this mansion would be restored to its former glory.

Before we entered the mansion, Susan gave me a personal tour of the grounds which supposedly included a pet cemetery, although the exact location of the gravesites remained unknown. While we walked down the narrow wooded paths that encircle the 500-acre property, I caught a glimpse of the back of the mansion through the bare wooden branches. What Hollywood producer wouldn't give his or her right arm to shoot a ghost movie here?

As we crept out of the woods and walked towards the front door, I was overcome with excitement and fear. Never before had I toured a property such as this!

Susan unlocked the door and we entered through the dark front hall. The silence was shattered by the slam of the door behind us. The air inside was heavy and cold. Quite a few windows were boarded shut, and parts of the house were enveloped in an eerie blanket of darkness. As we walked from room to room, Susan pointed out that much of the beauty had been lost due to water damage and vandalism, but the structural integrity remained intact. In fact, throughout the tour there wasn't a single squeak from the hardwood floors. The interior featured many lavish and ornate touches, with many fireplaces throughout decorated with hand-painted tiles. After a while, I began to realize how easy it would have been to get lost in the place, as one room led into another. Even the servants quarters were extensive.

I had to admit there were parts of the house that gave me an uneasy feeling, and occasionally a strange noise would emanate from some part of the house. I couldn't imagine how frightening it would have been to spend the night alone here. But I also couldn't imagine not wanting to.

After the tour I was anxious to hear about the mansion's haunted history, but the air was getting so cold inside it became unbearable. It was almost as if the house was politely asking us to leave. So we did.

I conducted the rest of the interview outside where Susan went into some detail about the house. In 1878 a man named Pierson Beebe built this three-story mansion as a summer residence. It was modeled after the British Pavilion at the Philadelphia Exposition in 1876. The architecture is Queen Anne stick style, which is a melding of European and American styles. There are seven chimneys and

16 fireplaces. The last member of the Beebe family associated with the town of Falmouth died in 1932. The house changed hands several times after that. In 1952 a Texas oilman purchased it, adding the plantation style front. He summered there until his death in the early 1960s. The property was next acquired by a group of local people who planned to clear the land and build 500 new houses. At that point, J. K. Lilly III stepped in and purchased the entire property, donating the land to the town of Falmouth and other organizations, including the local hospital, the Falmouth Academy and the Cape Cod Conservatory of Music and Art.

During the 1970s, the house was sporadically inhabited. In the 1980s, decay set in and it has remained essentially vacant ever since.

The hauntings date as far back as the 1950s. Susan remembered speaking to a man who used to summer there during that time period. At first, he had been reluctant to share his experiences with her, saying only that he was a rational person who didn't believe in ghosts. However, after a while he began to change his tune, and he told Susan about two experiences he had at the mansion.

The man was the nephew of the Texas oilman who owned the house during the 1950s. During his college years, he invited a lady friend over to the house one weekend while his uncle was away. He and this woman were in the front room just off the formal parlor, with the doors closed. In his own words, they were "making out" when both of them began to hear loud footsteps walking down the main staircase. It apparently sounded like a woman walking in heels. The footsteps made their way down the staircase and stopped in front of the door of the front room. The couple was paralyzed with fear, afraid to move even an inch. The entity stayed in front of the door for a couple of minutes, then turned and walked back up the staircase. When they got up the nerve to open the door, they searched the entire house, but could find no one. The man said it had a chilling effect on both of them.

Some years later, this same man had an even more remarkable ghostly encounter at Highfield Hall. Just after a major hurricane hit the Cape, his uncle requested that he drive down and inspect the property for damage. The whole Cape was without electricity and he arrived after dark, with the wind still howling but the night sky just beginning to clear. He unlocked the front door, walked in and was astonished to see a woman hovering above the staircase landing. The apparition started down the staircase toward him. Gripped with fear, he fled the house and did not return until daylight. He was so shaken that he brought someone with him upon his return.

Susan believes that the ghostly entity may have been Mary Louisa Beebe or possibly Emily Beebe, sisters of Pierson Beebe. Mary Louisa did not live in the house on a regular basis, but visited her siblings quite often. She was the world traveler of the family and the most fashionable. Emily, on the other hand, lived in the house and was said to be a meticulous housekeeper. Susan remarked that Emily would be extremely unhappy with the present condition of the house.

There have been rumors of others seeing ghostly apparitions in the house as well. Some have reported seeing human figures in one particular window on the second floor. Susan confessed that even she has heard eerie noises in the mansion while alone. But that's not all she has experienced. In our next chapter you will read about an unexplainable occurrence that she personally witnessed involving an alarm, a door and a police officer.

Psychic Cop at the Haunted Mansion

n the words of a 20-year police veteran, Michael McGillvary:

As you know, I was a Falmouth Police officer for twenty years. I remember one evening being dispatched to Highfield Hall because the alarm had been activated. I had been informed that a new alarm system had just been installed in the building. When I arrived, I met the director, Susan Shephard. We entered the building together and started looking around. We walked around the first floor and then investigated the second floor, but everything seemed to be okay.

When we got to the third floor, I noticed every door was open except for one. I walked up to the door and asked Susan if there was any reason why this one particular door was closed. She told me that all the doors in the building are always supposed to be left open. She had absolutely no idea why that door was closed. I grabbed the doorknob and tried to turn it, but the door wouldn't open. I then began to lightly push on the door. I told Susan that it felt like the door was locked. Susan then began to try to open the door herself. She pushed and shoved, but the door refused to open.

By now Susan was getting a little nervous. I told her we had two options. We could either try to find a key or I could kick it open. I was starting to get concerned that maybe someone was in the building and they had locked themselves in that room. Susan said there was no key to that room and was trying to decide if she wanted me to kick the door in. I walked back over to the door and this time I really put my shoulder into it and it still wouldn't budge. Once again we began to talk about what to do. Susan walked over to the door to give it one last try. When she turned the knob the door flew out of her hand and swung open by itself! The two of us just looked at each other. I walked into the room to investigate but of course no one was there, and I knew it would have been virtually impossible for anyone to have escaped because we were on the third floor and it's a long way down.

I began to sense the presence of an elderly man in the room and felt that it must have been his room at one time. I believe the man felt we were trespassing on his space and he had been the one holding the door closed. In time he came to realize that we were going to enter the room one way or another and instead of having his door kicked in, he decided to release it. The third floor used to be the servants quarters, and I sensed this man was not an actual servant, such as a waiter or butler, but rather someone that was in charge of the mansion's upkeep. The whole thing was really an incredible experience.

Psychic Cop at a Falmouth Inn

I n the words of a 20-year police veteran, Michael McGillvary:

One night in February I was working when the weather was less than ideal. A blizzard was raging and we had nearly white-out conditions. I was driving around in my police car with another member of the department who regularly rode with me at night. I was trying my best to keep the car on the road when I got a call to go to an inn in Falmouth. The station informed me that the caller was very upset and thought someone had broken into the inn and might still be there. When we arrived, the manager met us at the front door.

When you first walk through the front door of this grand old building you enter a large foyer and immediately to your right is a set of stairs which leads up to a landing where there is a second set of stairs leading up to the second floor. On the landing there is a seat built into the wall and just above the seat are little windows that overlook the front driveway. I believe there were four sets of windows and two of them were wide open, with snow blowing in. The manager also pointed out huge pillows that had been knocked off the seat and onto the floor. The pillows were so heavy, I think they probably weighed about five pounds each. It certainly looked like someone had in fact broken in.

I tried my best to calm the man down, but something kept telling me things were not as they appeared. As we continued to talk, I happened to notice there was dirt on the floor. It looked like someone had taken a handful of dirt, stood at the base of the second set of stairs and just flung it up the staircase. The dirt was heaviest at the base of the stairs and continued to get lighter as you walked up. Now I'm thinking, "This is getting really bizarre. There's a blizzard going on, the ground is covered with snow, where would the dirt have possibly come from?" I noticed there were two plants on each side of the seat. I figured this was the only place the dirt could have come from. I walked over to the first plant, but the dirt was undisturbed. I then walked over to the second plant, again the dirt was undisturbed.

I asked my colleague who was with me to take the manager and check out one part of the inn while I investigated another part. We all met back at the foyer but found absolutely nothing. The man really began to get nervous. He kept saying, "Where is this person hiding?" I tried once again to calm him down and said I was going to walk around the outside of the house. I told him to stay by the front door and scream if anything happened.

My friend and I walked around the entire house in knee-deep snow but the only footprints we could find were our own. My friend asked what I thought about the whole thing. I said, "If you want my honest opinion, I believe the house is haunted and I think the manager did something to upset the entities in the house."

My friend said, "You're not going to tell him the house is haunted are you?"

I said, "I don't know what to tell him." I thought to myself, "If I tell him the house is haunted and that I'm psychic he's going to call the station, there are probably going to be guys in white suits waiting for me and I'm going on a vacation." So I had to find a way of introducing what I knew into the conversation without getting myself into a jam.

I walked back into the house and up to the landing with the manager. I told him that we had walked around the entire perimeter of the house and didn't find any evidence that anyone had been out-

side other than us. I said, "Look, there's not even any evidence from snow on boots or shoes that would have been left on the landing, and the carpet isn't wet. I know it looks like someone broke in, but I have to tell you, I don't believe anyone did."

"Well how do you explain it?" the manager asked. I pointed to the small windows above the landing and explained that only a very small person such as a child could have climbed through. His theory was that someone had climbed up the tree near the window and broke in.

"Well, how do you explain the dirt all over the floor? Why would someone do that?" he asked.

"I don't know why someone would do that," I replied, "but look at these plants. Look at the dirt inside. It's completely undisturbed. Don't you think that's a little strange?"

"Well, if the dirt didn't come from the plants, where did it come from?" he said. "What's going on here? Tell me what you think," he kept asking.

I told him I didn't have an answer or at least not one that would make sense to him. I tried calming him down and reassured him that we had searched the entire house. The only thing I felt I could say was that maybe the wind did it, but I knew he wasn't buying it. We talked a little more and then he thanked us for coming out and trying to help. But he said he still didn't understand the whole thing. I tried to make a little joke out of it and said, "Do you believe in ghosts?" I started laughing and said, "I'm only kidding," but the manager said, "I don't want to hear anything about ghosts. Don't even mention something like that, I live in this house by myself."

Just before I left I told him that if he had any other problems to call the station, and I would come back as quick as I could. I started to reach for the door and the manager said, "Hey, do you think the house is really haunted? Do you think this is why all of this happened?" I said, "Well, in life anything is possible, but I'll take a chance and tell you something about myself that I share with very few people, especially when I'm working. I'm psychic and for me, ghosts are very much a part of my life. I feel that you did something to upset these spirits, exactly what I don't know, but they're making some sort of statement. If you have an open mind and think about all that you have seen it will make perfect sense." He said, "Well, thank you for everything," and I left, although I was a little nervous that he might call the station and complain.

I went back to the house the next day to ask if anything else had happened. He said that everything had been very quiet. The manager then opened the door for a conversation about the house being haunted. At first I was a little reluctant to share what I knew for fear of getting myself in any deeper but something told me it was okay.

I told him there were three entities in the house. One was an older man, and he really looked like what a typical sea captain would look like, with his beard and pipe. The two other entities were female. One was a large matronly woman, the other a younger woman, probably in her thirties. I felt the younger one did not want anyone to know that she was there and when people do become aware of her presence, she runs off into different rooms.

The larger woman I felt I connected deeply with. I believe she really took a liking to me. She made herself known to me when I was talking in the house and at one point she actually walked right into me. When this happened, I felt extremely cold, literally chilled right to the bone. I was freezing. When I left the house, I could feel this entity walking behind me and when I got in my car, I felt she was sitting beside me. I had never had a ghost enter my car before. Not really knowing what to do, I began to drive and when I got about a half-mile away from the house, she disappeared. I guessed they must be constrained by certain distances.

The manager eventually became more comfortable talking about the subject and admitted that he has had some strange experiences in the house. He told me that at night, he has heard unexplainable noises, such as people walking around or mysterious voices. Once he accepted that these ghosts might be real, he began to feel more comfortable in the house and he never had a problem again.

Hidden World

THE NIMROD RESTAURANT

This hole in the wall at the Nimrod Restaurant was made by a British cannonball during the War of 1812 that was shot from the British ship, *The Nimrod*, for which the property was named. The cannonball shown here is reported to have come from *The Nimrod* as well, although it is not the actual ball that did the damage.

If you're searching for an historic restaurant serving mouth-watering traditional New England cuisine, and you wouldn't mind having a ghost story or two on the side, the Nimrod Restaurant is for you.

The Nimrod was originally two separate homes. The smaller home was built in the 17th century and was originally situated on Old Falmouth Harbour. It had been hit by cannon fire in 1814 from the British ship *H.M.S. Nimrod* during the War of 1812, hence the name of the restaurant. The second home was considerably larger, built in the 18th century and located on Main Street.

In 1922 both houses were moved on rollers by eight horses to their present location. The structures served as a private home for many years until they were converted to a guesthouse and named the Boxwood Inn. During the 1950s, the inn was turned into a semi-private club known as the Nimrod Club and operated as such until the 1970s. After careful renovations the current structure has been transformed into one of Cape Cod's most unique restaurants and is presently owned and operated by James and Gwyn Murray. The original hole in the wall that was caused by cannon fire has been preserved to this day and can be viewed in the men's room. As I told you, this is one of Cape Cod's most unique restaurants.

It has been documented that the building was used to hide slaves in the 1800s as part of the Underground Railroad which helped lead them to freedom in Canada, and there are in fact many secret hiding places throughout the structure.

In one part of the restaurant there is an old staircase leading up to a small room that is now sealed over by a wall. Years ago, when the staircase was in use, some people claim they had seen apparitions of slaves at the top of the staircase. In fact, one previous owner had his office in that room. On more than one occasion, he sensed a strong presence while walking up the stairway. Each time this happened, he would find an old door leading to a sleeping loft (where slaves were supposedly secreted) was wide open. At that point an apparition of an elderly black man would often appear to him. He believes the ghost to be a former slave.

The cellar seems to be another place for heightened paranormal activity. Down one of the long dark corridors employees have often reported hearing someone walking behind them, even when they were certain they were alone. Owner Jim Murray has experienced these footsteps in the cellar firsthand. He has also seen eerie, dark human-like shadows pass by him in the corridor. Once he remembers being so convinced that one of his employees was in the next room that he actually began speaking to the employee, only to find out a few seconds later that he was in fact alone. To this day there are those who refuse to go into the dark cellar altogether.

On the second floor there are several small rooms in which some employees reside. Bizarre happenings have been reported here as well. I spoke to a woman who said while she was sleeping her hair dryer, which was plugged in, suddenly flew off of the nightstand, crashed to the floor and then turned on by itself.

As you can plainly see, there is no shortage of ghostly tales at the Nimrod Restaurant.

THE NIMROD RESTAURANT
FALMOUTH, MASSACHUSETTS
508-540-4132

Ghostly Ooze

GAS LIGHT INN

I must admit it was the name of this inn that first caught my attention. How could a property called the Gas Light Inn not have a ghost? I simply had to find out. When I first called innkeeper Frank Mendola, he seemed a little surprised by my questions; but after filling me in on the inn's history, he invited me down for a more in-depth interview.

After seeing this Victorian inn for the first time, I had a little trouble focusing on the hauntings that have taken place here. The reason being is that the Gas Light Inn is just so beautiful. It's easy to understand why the same guests return year after year. For starters it features an enormous wrap-around porch with sweeping views of

Martha's Vineyard. The large front parlor is lavishly decorated with exquisite hand-picked Victorian pieces. Just off the front parlor you'll find the spacious dining room where a full breakfast is always served on fine English china. The three oversized guestrooms all have ocean views, and each is lovingly decorated with Victorian furniture and interesting antiques.

The inn dates back to 1880. It was constructed by men who built whaling vessels that left port from Falmouth and Woods Hole. The golden age of whaling in Falmouth dates between 1820 and 1865. The Gas Light Inn is now owned and operated by Frank, a retired police officer, and his energetic wife, Diane Mendola, a retired nurse. They are originally from Brooklyn, New York.

Diane told me that it was not long after they purchased the Gas Light that unexplainable events began to take place. The first report came from a gentleman who said he felt a strong presence while upstairs in a guestroom known as the Captain's Room. This same man said he also saw the figure of a woman at the top of the stairs peering out the window. He said the woman scurried away from the window and then suddenly vanished. He described her as being small, in her early twenties and wearing a blue dress. Diane asked the guest if he felt any fear. He replied no, but nevertheless refused to go upstairs. After that incident, Diane started noticing an indentation in the bed in the room where the presence had been felt. Diane said, "Every time I walked into the Captain's Room, I saw what looked like the indentation of a small person sitting on the bed." Frank also witnessed this strange occurrence. He insisted, "You could actually see two little buns with hand prints on both sides." This happened for quite some time and then suddenly stopped.

Diane said that the day after I initially called Frank and made my inquiries, she saw the same indentation once again, but this time it was on a bed in a room they call the Turret Room.

Still, the Captain's Room certainly seems to be the most active room in the house. Lights turn on and off without warning. Candlesticks move across the room, and even furniture is occasionally rearranged. Light footsteps, the kind a child or small woman would make, are sometimes heard coming from the room as well.

The Mendolas have even smelled pipe tobacco coming from the Captain's Room when no one was around.

The previous owner informed Frank and Diane that she, too, had sensed the presence of a woman. This owner went on to say that she remembered twice seeing a woman at the top of the stairs staring out of the window. She even heard light footsteps as the woman walked away.

The most memorable occurrence at the Gas Light did not actually happen in the Captain's Room but in the dining room. On a certain day Diane dusted and cleaned the china cups that are always on display in the dining room. She knows she cleaned on this particular day, because a friend who owns a nearby inn had called her at the time and asked why she was out of breathe, and she told the friend what she had been doing.

The next morning Diane came downstairs for a cup of coffee, and when she walked into the dining room, she could not believe her eyes. The china that was on her server and the wall behind it were covered in a thick, brown sticky ooze, almost like molasses. Diane said cups were stuck to saucers, and the saucers were stuck to the server. The wallpaper and mirror behind the server were drenched in this syrupy mess. Diane called to Frank and said in an accusatory tone, "Frank, what did you do here?" "I didn't do anything," Frank replied. At the time the inn was vacant which only added to the mystery.

Diane quickly grabbed the phone and called the friend that she had spoken to the day before. Both the friend and her husband came running over. "This can't be, you just cleaned all of that yesterday. I was on the phone with you yesterday while you were cleaning," exclaimed the friend. Diane thought it was also strange that whatever the ooze was, it cleaned up remarkably easily, without even leaving a stain on her wallpaper.

Fortunately Diane and Frank feel that the spirits that haunt the Gas Light Inn are benign and mean no harm. "After nine years you just get used to it. I mean that. You just accept it," said Diane.

GAS LIGHT INN
FALMOUTH, MASSACHUSETTS
508-457-1647

The
ISLANDS

"Put That Back, It's Mine!"

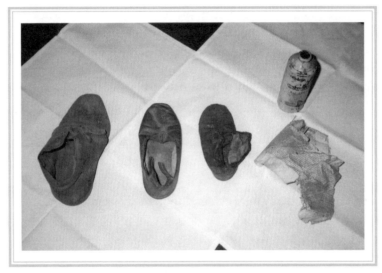

Items found on property.

I have often been asked, "Do you have a favorite inn?" or, "What town do you like best?" I will respond to the first question by saying that every inn I have included in this book I hold near and dear to my heart. The simple truth is I really have no favorite. On the other hand, I do have a favorite town and it happens to be the one I am currently writing about.

Edgartown on Martha's Vineyard is rejuvenation for the soul. I can think of nothing more enjoyable than strolling its narrow flower-laden streets or gazing upon its gracious sea captains' homes. It is an unspoiled gem, glistening by the sea.

Just a short jaunt from Edgartown Harbor, beyond the quaint shops, brings us to a classic 19th century inn. It is an interesting blend of historic and contemporary flavors. The front sitting room is a mix of unusual antiques and comfortable contemporary furnishings. The 14 guestrooms are all bright and cheerful, and the flower-filled courtyards are wonderful for relaxing, as is the inviting front porch.

Innkeeper Sarah Grady is a joy to be with and always wears a smile. Sarah informed me that during recent renovations of the inn, workers found old newspapers dating back to the 1790s, children's marbles, and six very old little girls' shoes, made of leather.
Sarah and her staff believe the inn may be haunted by the spirit of a playful little girl. Sarah said that one time a couple staying in Room 3 reported hearing someone walking up and down the stairs all night. At the time the inn was completely empty. Room 3 in particular seems to be the center of the inn's ghostly activity.

Once while doing some renovations in Room 3, a startled painter dropped his paintbrush and took three steps toward the hall. He called out to Sarah who he hoped was playing a trick on him. Sarah came walking out of another guestroom. "You weren't just over there!?" he exclaimed. The painter reported seeing a dark shadow float across the hallway and disappear. Sarah stated that other people including herself have witnessed this dark figureless shadow floating across Room 3, particularly in winter. Some guests have even seen shadow-like feet under the door. Chambermaids have also reported neatly putting things away only to come back and find everything rearranged.

One of the inn's employees, Karen Anderson, told me about some strange incidents that had happened to her just two days before I first visited them. During a routine cleaning of Room 3, Karen discovered an antique hairpin in a side drawer next to the bed. She found this quite ironic since she had just finished reading the night before about another haunted inn on Martha's Vineyard and the staff's experiences with old hairpins.

Karen removed the hairpin from the drawer and carried it upstairs to Room 7, which was next on her list to clean. Before she started she wanted to show Sarah the unusual hairpin she had found. The moment Karen stepped out of Room 7, the hairpin was suddenly plucked from her hand and mysteriously vanished. Karen said, "It felt like someone just knocked it out of my hand." Thinking it must have landed somewhere on the floor she began an endless search. The hairpin was nowhere to be found. At that point she walked downstairs and began searching Room 3. Karen decided to check the bedside drawer where she had originally found the object. As she slowly pulled open the drawer she found herself staring at the little antique hairpin. It was almost as if an angry little girl had spoken to Karen and said, "Put that back, it's mine!"

Authors note: Shortly before this story first went to press, the owners if the inn became a little nervous – well, very nervous – about using the inn's real name. They requested that I change the name of the inn as well as the names of the employees.

You'll have to find this one on your own!

Oh, Ellie!

THE EDGARTOWN INN

ask you, what could be more wholesome than munching chocolate chip cookies on the porch of the Edgartown Inn during the town's festive Fourth of July parade? I've always wanted to visit Edgartown during the Fourth of July, so I was very grateful to do so recently while investigating a ghostly presence called Ellie. It's a nice place to call home, even just for a few days.

This stately property was constructed in 1798 as a residence by Captain Thomas Worth. His son William Jenkins Worth was noted as being a hero in the Mexican War, and Fort Worth, Texas was named after him. As time passed, the captain's home was transformed from a residence to an inn and named the Gibbs House.

It then changed to the Norton House and finally became the Edgartown Inn.

The inn has hosted many notable guests such as Daniel Webster, who was initially denied lodging because he was dark-skinned and thought to be of Native American descent. Nathaniel Hawthorne was also a frequent guest, working on his short story collection *Twice Told Tales* during his stay. Other famous guests have included Charles Summer, a 19th century opponent of slavery, and John F. Kennedy while he was still a Massachusetts senator.

Today the Edgartown Inn rests under the watchful eye of innkeeper Sandi Hakala. The inn features 12 cozy guestrooms; a magnificent, richly decorated front parlor; and a spacious front porch adorned with comfortable white wicker furniture.

So is there a ghost at the Edgartown Inn? Well, according to Sandi there have been some inexplicable happenings. Sandi recalled a time when two women were staying in a guestroom known as the Major Worth Room. One of the two women came down for break-fast, wide-eyed and pale, and asked if anyone had ever seen a ghost in the house. Sandi mentioned to her that someone had in fact reported seeing a ghost, and it happened to have been in the Major Worth Room. The woman went pale again and said that she saw a ghost in her room the previous night.

She explained how she woke up in the middle of the night and witnessed a very thin woman dressed in white with long flowing gray hair, standing at the foot of her bed and attempting to make the bed with her in it! She said she immediately turned on the light, which woke her friend who was sleeping in the other twin bed, but then the apparition vanished. Her friend chalked it up to one too many beers and told her to go back to sleep. The woman said she tried to go back to sleep but couldn't. Suddenly, she found herself staring at the ghostly apparition again, who was still attempting to make her bed.

Shortly after these two women checked out, Sandi, along with another manager and caretaker named Henry, had a discussion about who this ghost may be. They concluded it must be Ellie, a disgruntled chambermaid who worked with Henry approximately 30 years previously. She was much older than Henry and probably in

her nineties when she was fired for the simple reason that her age prevented her from adequately performing her duties. Needless to say, Ellie was not happy. Sandi mentioned that during the discussion Henry's ill feelings for Ellie surfaced. He started making quite a few derogatory comments about her.

Later on in the day, after the meeting was adjourned, Henry was walking past the Major Worth Room, where a plaque hung that had been awarded to Henry for his fifty years of hospitality. The very moment he walked by the plaque it dropped from the wall to his feet, with glass shattering everywhere!

Sandi confessed that she as well as other employees have felt a strong presence, particularly in the downstairs office, during the off season or periods when things have quieted down.

The above pretty much summarizes the information I was able to glean through interviews about the paranormal at the Edgartown Inn, but don't forget that I too was a guest there! It may have been nothing, who knows? But the first and only time my tape recorder has ever malfunctioned occurred at the Edgartown Inn. What's more, it wasn't just a little malfunction. One of my tapes wound into a terrible mess, forcing me to redo my interviews at the Edgartown

Inn and ruining my recording of a story I had heard elsewhere on the island! I'm tempted to write the whole thing off as an everyday mechanical problem, but there was just something about it that left me thinking that I had laughed just a little too hard at some of the wisecracks that were made about a 90-year-old chambermaid. As I exited the inn to head back to Cape Cod, all I could think was, "Oh, Ellie!"

THE EDGARTOWN INN

EDGARTOWN, MASSACHUSETTS

508-627-4794

Laddie and the
One-Armed Ghost

THE DAGGETT HOUSE INN

Secret staircase at The Daggett House

The Daggett House is noted as being the first tavern on Martha's Vineyard licensed to sell beer and ale. Way back in 1660, taverner John Daggett was fined five shillings for selling strong liquor.

Over the centuries, the Daggett House has served as a store, a boarding house for sailors, and a counting house during the whaling days. In 1948 the property was purchased by Mr. and Mrs. Fred Chirgwin and established as a bed and breakfast. The Daggett House currently encompasses four distinct properties. The main house boasts five guestrooms, two suites, a traditionally decorated front parlor and a restaurant. The delightful Garden Cottage, with its scenic views, once served as a school and artist's studio; it now harbors three additional guestrooms. Across the street lies a 1780 Greek Revival Whaling Captain's home known as the Captain Warren House, where you will find 13 guestrooms and two suites. And on nearby Simpsons Lane stand the Henry Lyman Thomas House and Cottage, once home to the keeper of the lighthouse. Today it houses five junior suites and a separate lightkeeper's cottage.

Any guest staying at any of the Daggett House properties, whether for a couple of days or a couple of weeks, will surely leave with the fondest of memories.

The Daggett House even has a special little secret. Downstairs in the old tavern there is a particular old bookcase which, when pulled away, reveals a secret staircase. This staircase leads to one of the loveliest guestrooms on the island. Back in the 17th century people sometimes constructed houses with hidden chambers in order to lessen their tax burden, since properties were taxed on the number of rooms.

Of course, there are other secrets here as well ... ghostly ones. In fact, the Daggett House has one of the most haunted reputations on the Island. It all began back in the mid-18th century when the Daggett House was a private residence. Two little boys were living here along with their parents. One day their mother decided to send one of the boys up to Chilmark to visit his grandmother. Back then, getting from Edgartown to Chilmark was at least a half-day's journey by horse and buggy. Just before the boy left he decided to play a prank on his brother. He took his brother's dog, named Laddie, and hid him in the secret staircase room. That night the other brother was so distraught over not being able to find his dog that he ran out in the pouring rain hollering, "Laddie! Laddie!"

But Laddie was not to be found. The next day, the boy became very ill and died a few days later of pneumonia. When his grieving mother eventually opened the secret staircase room, she found Laddie, paws up and stiff as a board. He had died of starvation. When the other brother returned from his grandmother's house, he was told what had happened. After hearing the news, the boy felt so guilty that he ran in back of the house, threw himself into the harbor and drowned!

With a history like this, it is no wonder that the staff as well as some guests have reported strange happenings in the secret room. People have reported hearing boys giggling, while others have reported hearing a dog whimper and seeing paw prints on the floor. In an attempt to sooth Laddie's spirit, dog biscuits are usually left in the room by staff members.

In another part of the inn, in a room called the Chappaquiddick Suite, a guest reported seeing an apparition of a woman who extended her hand and touched the guest's forehead. The guest said that she had never experienced such a peaceful sensation in her life.

Back in the 1940s, a photo was taken of the old beehive fireplace in the tavern. When the photo was developed something very strange was discovered. In the flames of the fire, an uncanny resemblance of a little boy's face appeared along with the outline of a dog. This photo is now on display at the inn.

In the cozy tavern, we will hear of another ghost that haunts this inn, commonly referred to as the one-armed man. George, a member of the inn's wait staff, tells the story as follows:

Well, actually the first time anything happened was when I first started working here about six years ago. Someone had sent me up to the attic to get something they needed. I had never been up there before, and I was a bit leery to begin with because I'm a little claustrophobic. So anyway, I walked up to the top of the very narrow staircase and stepped into the room. Directly in front of me was a man, probably about six feet away from me. I didn't move. I simply stared at him and he stared back at me. Then I thought, "Surely it must be me. It's probably the sun casting a shadow or something."

Well, low and behold, there was a man standing there. He was rather tall, with very long hair and was missing an arm. He wasn't doing anything, just sort of smiling. I'm not sure how much time went by, it could have been twenty seconds or a minute, when all of a sudden an extremely bright aura appeared around his body. It became so bright that I actually had to look away. It looked like tiny white lights surrounding his body. After I looked away, I tried to look back at him, but suddenly he went backwards and everything began to twinkle around him. He was gone. I just stood there. I then grabbed what I had come up for and left. I never said anything about this incident for three months.

The same man has appeared to me several times since then. He has appeared at my apartment as well as at work. One time when it was really late, I was working here alone with no houseguests. It was late in the fall and I was doing some paperwork when I began to hear footsteps. I had just recently checked the building and was certain I was the only one here. So, I listened as the footsteps came down the stairs and heard the final footstep hit the floor. I slowly turned and standing before me was the same man. As soon as he saw me, he went flying across the hallway and then just vanished.

As I mentioned, I've also seen him in my apartment. One afternoon I was due at work at 4:00 P.M. I always lie down to rest just before going to work. I was resting on the couch, not sleeping, but just lying there when I was overcome with the feeling that someone was outside my apartment door. Now, I'm lying there thinking, if someone's there, why aren't they knocking? The next thing I know, he is standing right by my couch, just standing there. I immediately sat up and his left hand went right across my face, and then he just disappeared.

Another time I was walking home from the post office, when for some reason I was compelled to look up at my living room windows. In the left window I saw his hand and his long white fingers seemed to be adjusting my fan. When I walked up to my apartment door, I didn't see him, but when I entered I felt him walk past me.

George had one more interesting story; but if you recall in the previous chapter, "something" played havoc with my tape recorder, and it was this story by George that was destroyed. So, I will have to tell it in my own words, as best as I can remember. "Oh, Ellie!"

One day out of nowhere George had someone's name pop into his head. The name was Ephram. He had absolutely no explanation as to why. George had never even heard of the name Ephram before. Shortly thereafter, he was chatting with two guests and inquired if they had done anything interesting while on the island. The couple said they had just returned from touring an old cemetery in Oak Bluffs. On one of the tombstones they saw a name and they wondered if it had any connection with the inn. The name on the tombstone was Ephram Daggett.

THE DAGGETT HOUSE INN

EDGARTOWN, MASSACHUSETTS
508-627-4600
800-946-3400

The Redheaded Woman

SHERBURNE INN

The Sherburne Inn on Nantucket was constructed in 1835. At the time it was headquarters for the Atlantic Silk Company, owned by William H. Gardner, Samuel B. Tuck and William Coffin. The company possessed one of the only two power looms in the world. Hard times hit the silk factory, and by 1844 it was no longer in operation. In the mid-1800s, the factory was divided into two separate units, the east side having been converted into a guesthouse, presently the Sherburne Inn.

Over time the inn has changed owners many times, eventually making its way into the capable hands of Susan Gasparich and Dale Hamilton. This magnificent Greek Revival has been restored with exquisite taste.

When Susan and Dale purchased the inn in March of 1994, they were informed by the previous owners that the inn was haunted. They said a former owner had reported seeing a woman dressed in Victorian garb, wearing a white dress, with long red hair. Dale and Susan commented that shortly after they became inn-keepers bizarre events started happening.

A guest staying in one of the rooms told Susan that at approximately two in the morning she was awakened by what she described as a "passage of someone." She described seeing a misty, cloud-like figure float by. In the morning she said to her husband, "I must have had a dream last night." While she was describing her experience to him, he said that he, too, had awakened at around two and saw the very same cloud-like image. Apparently neither of them knew the other was awake.

A gentleman staying in a different room said he was in the bathroom about to shower when he noticed the old-fashioned lock on the door. He clearly remembers the old latch being in the unlocked position before he stepped into the shower. When he came out the latch had been thrown into the locked position. One guest, after being locked out on the balcony of his room, had to yell for someone to let him in.

Susan thinks the ghost is a bit of a trickster but quite harmless. The strange presence that is often felt by her and certain guests is one of peacefulness and tranquility, certainly nothing of a malevolent nature.

That being said, a couple staying in Room 5 told Susan of a rather hair-raising experience they had endured one evening. In the middle of the night the couple awoke to a strange and frightening noise. The sound of long fingernails starting at the top of the wall and slowly scratching their way down echoed in their room. It happened over and over again, fingernails slowly scratching from top to bottom. The couple did not investigate.

Who this ghost is, most certainly is anyone's guess. Dale and Susan speculate there might be a connection to the old silk factory, but no one really knows.

Sherburne Inn
Nantucket Island, Massachusetts
508-228-4425

The Oldest Inn
on Nantucket

THE WOODBOX INN

Some inns are known for their fine cuisine and award-winning wines, while others receive recognition for their quaint atmosphere and gracious hospitality. Few can claim all of the above, but The Woodbox Inn can do just that.

Imagine the owner of a thriving inn and restaurant on Nantucket at the height of the season willing to sit down and discuss ghost stories with a writer. That's more than I can say for a number of other establishments who said, "Oh, you've got to be kidding!" or, "I'm in the middle of serving tea, and I don't have time to speak to writers this time of year!"

One woman was so irate that I would dare disturb her, that she gave me a thorough verbal thrashing about how I should not call inns this time of year and how she didn't even have 10 seconds. Although, I must say, she took more than 20 minutes to tell me off, which is the average length of an initial interview. After responses like that, the words of Woodbox owner Dexter Tutein were music to my ears: "Stop by anytime in the morning, just give me a call a few minutes before to make sure I'm here."

I could easily go on about the inn's intimate décor and charming guestrooms, but what made my visit so memorable was the employees who put their heart and soul into their work and showed such great affection for one another. By the time I had completed my research, I felt so good that I really didn't want to leave.

Apparently I'm not alone, as there are others who do not wish to leave this 18th century house, either. These are the spirits that reside at the Woodbox Inn. History reveals the main building was constructed by Captain George Bunker in 1709. The adjoining house was built by his brother in 1711. An interior staircase now joins the two houses together. The Bunker family owned the property until the 1920s, when it was purchased by Maude Stovell and converted into an antique shop, inn and tearoom. It was then purchased by Dexter's mother, Marie Tutein, in the 1950s.

The inn is thought to be haunted by several different entities: a sea captain who appears in uniform, a little girl and a young woman, among others.

The staff at the inn was most willing to chat about their ghostly experiences, and a good place to begin is with a lovely woman named Yvonne:

It was about three years ago. My daughter was three-and-a-half years old. She was playing in one of the empty guestrooms upstairs while I was downstairs cleaning up. I noticed it was very quiet in the room that she was playing in, so I went upstairs and asked her what she was doing. She said she was just playing, but I knew she wasn't telling me something. I also knew that people have seen a little girl and a young woman in that room. I asked my daughter if she was playing with the little girl, and she said yes. I then asked her what she looked like. My daughter said that she was about her height with long blonde hair and was wearing a funky dress. The next day my daughter asked if she could come back and play with the little girl, but this time the little girl didn't return.

My own ghostly experience happened back in 1992 when I was living upstairs. While I was sleeping, I would sometimes feel someone's hand go through my hair. I would also hear fingers scratching on the mattress. I never saw anyone, but I definitely felt a presence. I assume it was the little girl playing with me.

Yvonne also told me about a dishwasher's experience at the inn. One night at about two in the morning, he was sitting at the owner's desk talking on the phone with his girlfriend. He looked up and noticed a bag hanging on the wall that a guest had forgotten. Suddenly the bag began to sway back and forth and then a ghostly figure of an older, heavyset woman dressed in black walked through the dining room and disappeared. He told Yvonne he was so scared that he literally threw the phone in the air.

The next person I had the pleasure of interviewing was a woman named Geri:

It was two years ago. I was living in a small room in the back. It is directly under a guestroom called the apartment. One night I woke up to the sound of footsteps above. It was late fall and I knew there weren't any guests in that room, but thought maybe it was someone who worked here. The next morning I asked if anyone had been upstairs in the apartment last night, but everyone said no. These were not light footsteps that I heard; they were heavy and it sounded as if two people were walking around. I have never seen anything here, but that night I know there were people walking around in that room.

The Woodbox Inn's friendly, outgoing chef, Bobby, also relayed his experience:

I started working at the Inn in the summer of 1980. It was my first summer on Nantucket, and I heard about people hearing and seeing strange things here. The first summer I didn't experience anything unusual. It wasn't until I came back to the island in 1983 as a chef that I began to have unusual experiences. In the morning, I would often be alone prepping in the kitchen when I would suddenly hear a little girl's voice calling my name. I would also hear footsteps and feel a breeze pass by. I had heard something about a little girl who once lived here and that she died of a fever years ago.

During one winter when they were jacking the floor up to do some foundation work, I remember crouching down to talk to the carpenter who was repairing the floor. Suddenly the carpenter turned white and said to me, "There's a guy standing behind you." I turned around and saw a tall, elderly gentleman in war-type Colonial clothing. He was clear as a bell, looking down at the two of us and smiling, and then he just disappeared. It was pretty strange.

I also interviewed another member of the inn's staff named Lina:

It was about three years ago. It doesn't seem very exciting now, but I was really very scared back then. I had never heard about ghosts at the Woodbox when I came to work here. I was living up in the attic and at night, when the lights were off, I would sometimes see a man dressed in a captain's uniform with a big hat starting at me by the door. He would never do anything, just stare. If I was frightened and had trouble sleeping, I would leave the lights on and he would never appear. I tried to talk to him and tell him not to come anymore, but he would never acknowledge me. He just continued to stare.

Despite her fear, Lina somehow just got used to this ghost's regular appearance. It's amazing what people can adapt to!

THE WOODBOX INN
NANTUCKET, MA
508-228-0587

Sightings

THE ROBERTS HOUSE INN

The Roberts House Inn and her sister properties, the Meeting House, Manor House and Linden House, are among Nantucket's finest lodging establishments. Located in the heart of picturesque Nantucket, rubbing elbows with quaint shops and gourmet restaurants, they are among the tall ships of Nantucket's inns, proudly under sail.

One might expect the proprietors of such lucrative businesses to be difficult to reach, perhaps observing their businesses from luxurious homes somewhere. In reality, owner Mike O'Reilly is always close at hand in his office in the basement of the Roberts House with his daughter, Tracy, working hard by his side. Each property is distinct and has its own unique flavor. I assure you, you won't find paint peeling or crumbs strewn about. The inns are impeccably maintained and decorated with splendid antiques and other pieces selected by Mike's wife, Sara.

The lot the Roberts House now rests on was occupied by a postage stamp house that burned to the ground in the great fire of 1846. The land was eventually auctioned off and purchased by a real estate developer named William Hussey. Hussey built a house which he used as his private residence until his daughter, Alice, converted it into an inn in 1883. She operated it until 1898, when the property was purchased by John Roberts at auction. His three daughters ran the inn until 1960. He subsequently purchased the building next door, which was built as a Quaker Meeting House in 1850. Roberts converted the property into a restaurant and added the rooms above. In 1960 the property changed hands again, and in 1974 it was purchased by the O'Reilly family. The building next to the Meeting House, now known as the Manor House, was built in 1846 and was known as the Royal Manor. It was operated as an inn by the Royal Family until 1986, when it was purchased by the O'Reillys.

The two buildings that are pertinent to the ghostly side of this story are the Roberts House and the Manor House. The first recorded sighting took place at the Roberts House in 1977. An employee, while in the service area of the basement, reported seeing the ghostly image of a young woman. This employee described her as having long hair and wearing a long nightgown. A second sighting was reported by a different person on the third floor. Again, this person reported seeing a young woman with long hair and wearing a long nightgown.

The next ghostly sighting took place just down the street at the Manor House. During reconstruction, Mike's cousin was in the house doing some carpentry work. He was the sole worker in the building and that evening, before he left to grab a bite to eat, he distinctly remembered locking all of the doors. Upon his return, he was walking towards the house, when suddenly he glanced up at the second floor window and saw a female figure. He said that he was overcome with an eerie feeling, knowing that the building was locked and unsure who it could be. He searched the entire building, but could find no one.

In the same building, but in a different section, a guest reported feeling a presence nearby in the night, as if someone had floated around the bed.

Mike firmly believes that he is not sensitive to spirits. For as long as he has owned the inn, he has never witnessed any sort of paranormal happenings. "I don't know if any of these stories mean anything. I don't know if any of it did or didn't happen. I just know it was reported to me by different persons," said Mike.

THE ROBERTS HOUSE INN
NANTUCKET, MASSACHUSETTS
508-325-0750

The
MID·CAPE

Haunted Bookstore

ISAIAH THOMAS BOOKS & PRINTS

How could anyone write a book about haunted Cape Cod and not at least investigate the possibility of there being a haunted bookstore? James Visbeck, owner of Isaiah Thomas Books & Prints in Cotuit, tells me that tourists often stop by his shop just to photograph the lovely Italianate Victorian structure, which is drenched in a delicious shade of pink. But not to enter a bookstore such as this would be a terrible misdeed. Isaiah Thomas Books & Prints holds one of the finest collections of used and rare books on Cape Cod. One can easily become lost in a maze of paper and print encompassing almost every subject imaginable. It's helpful to have an owner with such a joyful personality and a willingness to educate his clientele. If reading is your cup of tea, this charming little bookshop is not to be missed, but don't be surprised if you sense something while ambling around here.

I conducted my interview with Jim while sitting on a comfortable, overstuffed couch that I am certain has caused many patrons to become sleepy-eyed, although I'm not positive loud snoring is encouraged. Jim turned down the classical music and we began to chat.

I was informed the house was constructed in the 1860s by a member of the Crocker family. Jim has a reproduction of an early photograph showing some of the family members sitting on the lawn in front of the house. Over time the house was transformed from a residence to a funeral home, a women's clothing store and a real estate office. At one time, the house was partitioned off and divided in half. Years ago, people would often rent the house for the summer months. Jim recalled a woman who came into the shop and told him that while she was a nursing student she and a friend rented part of the house for a few weeks during the summer. She told him a story about how her friend was doing some cleaning and suddenly fell down the narrow staircase and broke her knee. The woman said to her friend, "What happened? How did you fall down the stairs?" Her friend replied, "I didn't fall down the stairs, I was pushed!"

Even Jim has had some bizarre experiences in this house. For instance, there is a large, battery-operated clock that hangs on the wall behind the counter. On many occasions when he has been away for a period of time, the clock suddenly stops at the precise moment he walks through the door. Jim remains mystified by this phenomenon.

On the second floor, Jim has an apartment, which he shares with a friend. His friend has told him that he sometimes feels as if another person is sitting on his bed and will occasionally see a depression in the mattress.

One time Jim remembered receiving an article that someone had written pertaining to the ghost in the house. He immediately took the article upstairs for his friend to read. While he was reading it, the television set mysteriously turned on by itself, as if the ghost were trying to communicate in some way.

For some unknown reason Jim believes the spirit became quite angry once. The night they finally finished remodeling the upstairs, he heard a horrific noise at approximately 2:00 A.M. A row of glass bud vases came crashing to the floor. This incident was so disturbing that Jim said to the ghost, "All right, listen, no more of this stuff. No more throwing things around. You can stay here, but stop it." Evidently, the spirit must have been listening because it was the last time anything like that happened.

The most astounding experience to date happened to Jim while he was on the second floor. He was walking from his bedroom to the kitchen and suddenly saw a woman in white sitting on the sofa in the front room. He was so startled that he did a double take. The woman was not solid, but rather a ghostly transparent image that vanished instantly. He assumes this spirit may be one of the women in the old photo of the original family, which he keeps on display. If you gaze upon this haunting picture, you will notice that all the women are, in fact, dressed in white.

After I concluded, Jim encouraged me to do a little browsing. I was in one of the back rooms when a woman turned to me and said, "By the way, they're here. You're looking for ghosts aren't you? There's a spirit in the back room moving quickly back and forth, although I'm not certain as to why." Her daughter then turned to me and said, "My mother is in tune with these things. She can sense spirits!"

ISAIAH THOMAS BOOKS & PRINTS INC
COTUIT, MASSACHUSETTS
508-428-2752

Winifred and Friends

This sprawling 19th century mansion in Cotuit has one of Cape Cod's most haunted reputations. I interviewed one former owner of the home and a gentleman who house-sat the property during the 1970s. I'll begin with the house sitter, whom I'll refer to as John, as he does not wish to be identified.

John, a former journalist, had heard many stories about the house before he settled in during the winter. He was told the spirit of a woman named Winifred was responsible for many strange occurrences there. "When you're a journalist you're used to listening to everybody's stories with an open mind, but I really didn't pay much attention to them. Ghosts have never bothered me," said John.

He was informed that a small baby who was born to Winifred died in the house and that Winifred died shortly thereafter. The room that was the original nursery was eventually divided into two rooms, a linen closet and a bathroom. This section of the house is where many people, including John, have reported mysterious happenings. "There was clearly something very strange happening in the linen closet," John said. He often remembers walking into the closet and finding sheets and towels completely rearranged or thrown haplessly about. Heavy, unexplainable clumping noises were also periodically heard coming from the linen closet. He said that after a while he even began to sense the presence of another person living with him.

John remembers a time when a friend of his, who was a firm believer in the supernatural, came for a visit. He told John that he should have an exorcism to free the spirit. He explained to his friend that exorcisms were not his cup of tea. His friend then suggested that he offer the spirit something, perhaps a doll. Again, John declined. His friend then asked if he could at least see the linen closet. They both walked through the house and upstairs to the linen closet. The electricity had been turned off in that part of the home so they both carried flashlights. John opened the door to the linen closet and shined the light in. Resting on a pile of sheets was a doll that he had never seen before in his life. They just looked at the doll and left it there. The next day John went back to the closet to have another look, but the doll was nowhere to be found.

John recounted two other ghostly tales that involved infants. On one occasion, a friend came over with his young daughter for a visit. The child was getting sleepy so they put her to bed in John's room. Later that evening after his friend left with his daughter, John remembered something very strange happening. He woke up at some ungodly hour, almost frozen solid. He walked down to the main room only to find a large entry door wide open. This door was not prone to just swinging open, so John thought it was rather strange.

Later that winter John had a big party. One couple brought their infant daughter and he suggested they put her in bed in his room until they were ready to leave. For some unknown reason the couple didn't stay very long. When the party was over and John had gone to bed, the same thing happened. He awoke in the middle of the night freezing cold, only to find the same door off the main room wide open.

Years later John met up with the same couple that had attended the party with their infant daughter, who was now grown. Over dinner, they reminisced about the party and the old house. During the conversation, John brought up the story of Winifred, and as it turned out, the couple had never heard about John's experience with the open door in the middle of the night. After he concluded the story, the woman looked at her husband and asked him if he remembered why they had left the party so early that evening. Her husband had completely forgotten. The woman went on to say that when she went up to check on her daughter, she found the window in the bedroom wide open and the baby so cold she had turned blue. She scooped her up and told her husband they had to leave immediately, but for some reason they never told John about it.

About a week after the dinner, John decided to write an article for the newspaper he owned, documenting some of his ghostly experiences at the house. Shortly after the article was released, he received a phone call from a young girl who said she was the daughter of the new owners of the house. She politely asked if he would come over and tell her and her siblings about the ghost. John agreed and went over one afternoon. The woman who owned the house gave him a tour and showed him the renovations that had been completed. Suddenly, John realized they had removed the linen closet to make room for a spiral staircase. "You obliterated the linen closet, not a good thing to do," said John. The woman smiled and said she really didn't believe the house was haunted, but thanked him for coming over to entertain the children.

During the tour, the woman pointed out what child slept in which bedroom. John immediately noticed the bedroom that Winifred once slept in was unoccupied and asked why. She said they weren't sure about that room and told him one of their young daughters had tried to sleep in there but had become absolutely terrified. John tried to explain that maybe she had been frightened by the ghost, but again the woman refused to believe the house was haunted.

About a year later, John was driving by the house and noticed a "For Sale" sign out front. Another sign that said "Yard Sale" accompanied it. He pulled up to the house and noticed a large man in the yard. John had never met the woman's husband, so he walked over, introduced himself and asked if he was the owner. The man turned to him and said in an angry voice, "Oh, you're the one, you're the newspaper guy. You're not writing anything more about this house, are you?" John explained to the man that he had just sold the newspaper, and then asked what the problem was. The man went on to say the house was under agreement, and he didn't want the sale to fall through. John then asked why they were selling the house. The man replied in a thunderous voice, 'Because it's haunted!"

I was fortunate enough to track down one of the previous owners of the house, whose family owned the home for many years. When John spent those two years house-sitting it was for this woman's family. Her name is Jill. It is Jill's belief that there was more than one ghost that haunted her house. She said Winifred always made her feel good and that her spirit protected the home. However, there was one part of the house that did harbor quite a bit of negative energy, the old housekeeper's quarters. In fact, in the room directly above it, the air was so dead they called it the "dead room."

Jill said the house was full of ghostly activity. In one of the long hallways upstairs the sound of heavy footsteps could often be heard. She said the linen closet would often be found torn apart, and in the bathroom just off the linen closet some people have felt a pat while in the shower. Others have witnessed mysterious blue lights creeping down the wall and have heard doors open and close by themselves. Jill also mentioned that singing was sometimes heard coming from what had been the old nursery, and that in the front parlor the sound of people playing bridge could often be heard as well. It is a house she will truly never forget.

The Legend of Hannah Screecham

In the town of Cotiut, the legend of Hannah Screecham is still talked about to this day. Many years ago, when pirates roamed the New England shores, a woman named Hannah Screecham was said to live in a run-down cottage on a little spit of land overlooking Cotuit Bay.

She was a shriveled old woman with menacing black eyes, who wore a black cloak and walked with the help of a cane. Her laugh was said to have sounded like the piercing cry of a gull. She lived an isolated existence, coming into town only to stock up on food and supplies.

Over time the townspeople grew suspicious and frightened of her. Some thought she had supernatural powers and accused her of being a witch. When a group of prominent men journeyed out to her cottage, and demanded she leave the town, she flew into a terrible rage. The men reported the sudden appearance of several large and vicious dogs that came to her aid. The men retreated back to the village, but a week later when an epidemic of smallpox besieged the townspeople, it was decided that Hannah Screecham be taken from her home and tried for witchcraft. An angry mob gathered around the courthouse and in a matter of minutes took justice into their own hands, chasing Hannah out of the courtroom and into the street. The impatient mob dragged her to a large tree where a noose was put around her neck and she was hanged.

Just after she was hanged a pirate who had been sailing off the coast marched into the town with pistols drawn and cut the body of Hannah Screecham down. The pirate then carried the body off with two of his crewmembers. When the pirate was eventually captured he confessed that Hannah Screecham was his mother. He said he had buried a great treasure alongside his mother's body on an island known by the townspeople as Screecham's Island.

The treasure has never been found, but people have reported seeing a ghostly image of an old woman in black, skulking around the beach at sunset. To this day, some claim you can still hear her piercing cry.

Uncle Chester

In the words of an anonymous woman from Hyannis:

First of all, I want to say that I had never believed in ghosts. I was one of those people who said there's no such thing. People make these stories up. I don't accept them and I will never accept them.

I had been in the hospital to have an operation. My brother and his wife, Ruth, lived next door. At the time, they had Ruth's mother and father staying with them from Maine. It was around Thanksgiving and they had come down for the holiday. Since I had just come out of the hospital, my brother and his wife let me stay in their guest bedroom, while Ruth's mother and father stayed in my house. They would come over during the day and would return to my house to sleep.

My house had a business attached to it with an office. So the only people there during the day was a secretary or my brother who was in and out. One morning when I was recuperating, Edna, who was Ruth's mother, said to me, "You have a ghost in your house."

Edna was always kind of a kidder and she looked at me with this broad grin as if to see what I was going to say. I said, "Come on, stop pulling my leg! I don't have a ghost in my house."

She kept saying it until finally I said, "What makes you think I have a ghost in my house?"

Edna said, "When we went to bed last night there was a knocking on the wall. I knocked back and the ghost knocked back at me."

I told Edna, "It's fall and you probably had the heat turned on. I'm sure it's the water pipes needing to be vented."

Edna replied, *"Well, if you say so."*

I said, *"That's what I say, and that's what it is."*

Later on I started to think about it and I asked her exactly which bedroom and which bed she had slept in. I didn't say anything, but I thought to myself, *"There are no water pipes in the wall by the bed she slept in."*

Shortly after I forgot about the whole thing. Although I will say this, in the winter I would often sleep upstairs in the large bedroom with the walk-in closet in the back part of the house. Many a night, I would get the sense that there was someone in the room. In fact, I would often get goose bumps up and down my back for a second as I walked in the door. Sometimes I would actually turn on the closet light and look behind my clothes, the feeling was just that strong. Once in a while I would even bend down and look under the twin beds. I never did figure out what it was. I guess I just became used to it.

About three years later, I had to have an ear operation. After the operation I began to have terrible headaches. One summer night I was lying on the couch with the dog beside me. I woke up at around ten o'clock with the smell of pipe tobacco being blown in my face. It instantly woke me up, but I was still in kind of a daze. I sat up on the couch and thought to myself, *"What was that?"* It was a very strong smell of cherry tobacco. I noticed a window was open and the only thing I could think of was that someone must have been peeking in the window while smoking a pipe. I woke the dog up, put on his leash and walked around the entire house, but I didn't see anything. I thought obviously the man must have left, but I kept thinking to myself what a stupid person this must be to peek in someone's window while smoking that awful-smelling tobacco. I really felt as if someone were standing over me blowing directly into my face. I thought to myself, *"Holy mackerel! Someone should talk to that guy!"*

Some time after, I went on a trip for a week. I had a young fellow working with me in the office. My office was in the front of the house. It was a real estate business and there was another office in the back that was occupied by a builder. So, I went off to London *for a week in April, and Phil, the young man who was working for me, was watching over my business. When I returned home, he didn't mention anything out of the ordinary happening.*

As time went by, I eventually bought another house, the one I'm living in now. I relocated my business, so the only thing left in the old house was the builder's business. I closed it off from the main house, which I decided to rent, and moved my real estate business downtown. Ironically enough, I hired Edna's daughter and her husband to work for me in the business. Her name was Millie and she really believed in ghosts. She was into the spirit world and ESP.

I had rented out the house to a couple from Somerville for a year. The day the lease was up, they gave me the key back and off they went. Then I rented it out to another couple named George and Linda, along with Linda's three children. They moved in and just fell in love with the house. After a few months, they decided they liked the neighborhood and wanted to buy a house of their own. Millie took them out and showed them several properties. When they came back to the office, Millie looked at me with this big grin and said, "You have a ghost in your house."

I said, "Oh no, not this ghost thing again!" mainly because I knew her mother had told her about the knocking on the wall. So I walked into the conference room and thought to myself, "Don't tell me I have to go through this ghost business again. I'll find out what's going on. I'll put a stop to this foolishness."

I said, "Okay, Millie what's the story with this ghost?"

She said, "They will tell you."

Linda and George said, "Yes, it's true."

"What do you mean?" I said. "What's true?"

Linda said, "As you know, when I first saw your house I absolutely loved it. The day we moved in, we unpacked and put everything away. When we sat down in the dining room for dinner, we began to hear a lot of noise coming from upstairs: crashing, banging and slamming. I said to George, 'What was that?' George said, 'I don't know, but somebody must be upstairs.'"

Linda said they raced upstairs and found every picture and mirror they had hung on the walls smashed. The wires were still on the pictures and the hooks were still on the walls.

Linda said to George, "What could this be?"

George replied, "I think we have a ghost."

Linda said she was ready to cry. They cleaned up the mess, and the children were crying and saying that they didn't want a ghost in the house. Linda said she went to work the next day and told her boss about it. Her boss quieted her down and told her to relax and that maybe the ghost will get used to her and things will calm down.

Linda said, "We gave it a chance and decided to stay," but said to me, "You most certainly have a ghost and it is definitely a man."

I asked them how they knew it was a man. They both replied, "Because he smokes a pipe that smells like cherry tobacco and he blows it right into your face!"

I thought to myself, "Holy mackerel, that's what woke me up on the couch so many years ago, and I thought it was a Peeping Tom!" Linda then went on to say that George's father is friendly with Old Man Green, and they were going to invite him down to the house to conduct a séance. Old Man Green was a black man in his nineties who lived over by Chart House Villas, and apparently he has been holding these séances, or whatever they call them, to communicate with the otherworld for years.

I said, "Well, let me know what happens when he does it." But I have to tell you, I still wasn't accepting this.

So, for the next few days all Millie could do was talk about this ghost. Phil, the young man who was still working for me, said, "You know when you went to London that time?"

I said, "Yes."

Phil said, "When I was in the office on Saturday, I remember it being one of those cold, damp, windy April days. I was sitting at your desk, and I had an appointment with some people from Connecticut who never showed up. I heard somebody walk in the front door and walk up the stairs. I opened the two doors that separate the office from the front hall and staircase and yelled, 'The office is down here!' but there was no response. When I ran upstairs and turned the corner I heard a knocking on the wall."

I said to Phil, "Oh my God, which wall was it?" It turned out to be the same wall Edna heard the knocking on years ago. By the way, Phil had never heard that story about Edna's experience with the knocking. He then said he walked over to the bedroom and pushed the door open and said, "Alright, whoever's there, come on out!" But no one was there. He came out and quietly shut the door, and that's when he heard rattling coming from the big bedroom, the one I used to sleep in during the winter. He said he walked into that room and checked to see if a window had been left open, but found everything closed and locked. He closed the door, walked back downstairs and said to himself, "I'm getting out of here now!" Phil felt so foolish that he didn't tell me about this until everyone started talking about ghosts.

So anyway, George and Linda eventually got Old Man Green down to the house to communicate with the ghost. I was told that during the séance Old Man Green said it was my Uncle Chester, who was my father's brother. Evidently, he was trying to get a message to me. Old Man Green said he was also protecting my house. Whenever I was away and strangers were in the house, he would try to get rid of them. George and Linda said they would also hear doors opening and closing downstairs when they were trying to sleep, as if to drive them out.

I asked George and Linda what the message was [they had received at the séance]. *They explained that Uncle Chester felt that I wasn't utilizing my property to its fullest potential. Linda and George also mentioned that a presence of a woman had suddenly appeared during the séance. They said this woman had a habit of blowing perfume in your face.*

Well I started to think, "I don't know anything about ghosts, but they must have their reasons for being in my house." I know it wasn't my father because when I had the pipe tobacco blown in my face, my father was still alive, as well as my brother. My mother had passed away, but she wouldn't be smoking a pipe. I thought, "What other man would have a connection to my house that smokes a pipe?" I knew Uncle Chester helped build my house, which was originally my mother and father's. It had to be Uncle Chester, I thought.

The woman I wasn't sure about. I thought it was probably my mother. She would often dab on a little perfume behind her ears before she went out, and I knew she loved the house. Well, I left it at that.

I was told that during the seance, Old Man Green said the woman didn't have enough strength to communicate on her own. Old Man Green then looked at George and said, "Did you have a grandmother from Nantucket?"

George said, "No."

But Linda interrupted and said, "I had a grandmother from Nantucket."

Old Man Green said, "Well, this is your grandmother and she's trying to get a message to you. She left you a dinner bell in her will and she said you never received it."

Linda said, "That's right, when I was a little girl she would always let me jingle her dinner bell at lunchtime. She always said she would leave it for me, but I never got it." Old man Green said that she was very upset that Linda never received the dinner bell.

Well, let me tell you, after all of that, I was really starting to believe. Old Man Green then went on to say that Uncle Chester didn't like George and Linda's children. I guess he didn't like children at all. He said Uncle Chester spends most of his time sitting in the big bedroom at the back of the house. Apparently, Linda and George bought an antique loveseat from an auction and put it in the corner of that bedroom. They both told me that Uncle Chester just loved it. They said you could feel his presence sitting in the loveseat and smell the cherry pipe tobacco coming from it.

That winter Linda and George decided to have a party. I really can't remember if it was Christmas or New Year's. The children were told to play upstairs, but they were too afraid, saying that Uncle Chester was trying to drive them away by turning the lights out. George said to the children, "Let's go up and have a talk with him."

"Now, Uncle Chester, you leave these kids alone and you leave that light switch alone!" said George.

After that, everything stopped. Uncle Chester went into his bedroom and back to smoking his pipe. That night Uncle Chester must have been very nervous because Linda said when they went to bed, the room was filled up with so much pipe tobacco they could hardly breathe. Finally at about 3:00 A.M, George sat up in bed and screamed, "Uncle Chester, will you put out that G.D. pipe, you're driving us crazy!" Linda said, the tobacco smell instantly vanished, and the next day Uncle Chester was gone.

Well, that was it for Uncle Chester, except for one last thing. I remembered that he left a message for me that I wasn't utilizing my property to its fullest potential. I thought about it and thought about it. Along with my main house, I own six cottages. They were all rented out year-round, except for the front studio cottage, which used to be my father's office. So, I thought if I tried to rent the studio year-round, I would make quite a bit more money than just trying to rent it by the week in the summer. It would also give me a steady income. I went to talk to Craig, who was running the building business in the other part of my home. I said to him, "When you get a chance this spring, I want you to figure out how to winterize the front cottage so I can make it a year-round rental."

I remember one time Craig thought someone had broken into the house when he was alone in the office. He said the doors began rattling and banging like a hurricane was coming through. He had no idea it was Uncle Chester trying to drive him out.

Anyway, a few months later, I was in my office when the phone rang. It was Craig. He said, "You'll never guess what happened! I was in the office with my clipboard on my knee, and I was making notes on how to winterize your front cottage. While I was making notes, I happened to have been staring at a print on the wall, when my secretary Evelyn asked what I was doing. I told her I was making notes on how to winterize your cottage so you could make more money by renting it year-round. While I was talking to her, I was still looking at the print when all of a sudden, the print lifted off of the wall and gently floated to the floor."

Craig asked, "What do you think that was all about?" I said, "Craig, if you accept all these stories about Uncle Chester then you have your answer. That's his way of letting us know that I received his message, and that I'm doing something about it. What you also don't know is that print was one of the few things that I got from my Uncle Chester's house after he passed away."

The Barnstable Witch Project

I t is said the spirit of Liza Tower Hill, a reputed witch, haunts a 17th century house known as the Allyn House on the Old King's Highway.

Liza Tower Hill was born Elizabeth Lewis. She was later nicknamed Liza Tower Hill after the section of London that her husband's family originated from. Liza was born in the early 18th century. Her father was Benjamin Lewis, a farmer who built his house and raised his family in a secluded area near Crooked Pond in Barnstable. Liza was a bright but mischievous child, who was said to have never been afraid of the dark and who played in the forest without fear. She worked hard in the fields and seemed to know how to cure sick livestock. It was said that her laugh sounded like a bird, and that no harm ever came to her.

When Liza was seventeen years of age, she married a man named William Blatchford. The Blatchfords lived in a house in a remote part of town on the border of Halfway Pond, a mile west of the house in which she was born. She gave birth to eight children in her new house, during which time she also became rather isolated from the rest of Colonial Cape Cod. Townspeople of Barnstable and Sandwich claimed she somehow developed ties to the Evil One.

Some say that they saw her dancing on the surface of Halfway Pond with white flames surrounding her feet. It was believed that anyone walking on the Indian trail in the woods from Hyannis to Barnstable Harbor was exposed to Liza's spells. One woman claimed that while she was riding along the trail, Liza cast a spell on her horse. The horse refused to obey and kept circling Halfway Pond for long periods of time.

Another traveler, a man named Mr. Wood of West Barnstable, accused Liza of putting a bridle and saddle on him. He claimed she rode him many times to a pond known as Plum Pudding Pond in Plymouth. Apparently, witches gathered at night at Plum Pudding Pond.

An East Sandwich resident named Benjamin Goodspeed claimed that Liza forced him to act as her horse at night as well. He said he became so exhausted that he fled, boarding a ship that was heading out to sea. As he sailed farther and farther away from the haunted forest, the head of a black cat suddenly appeared in the water. It followed behind the vessel the entire day and at nightfall boarded the ship, taking the shape of Liza Tower Hill. She then rode the poor man until dawn, whereupon she turned back into a black cat and swam after the ship once again. A shipmate told Goodspeed to shoot the swimming cat with a double-barreled shotgun, using pages from the Bible for wads (wads were soft plugs used to hold the powder and shot in place.) Benjamin waited until night, and as soon as the cat began to climb aboard again he fired, hitting it in the head.

The cat fell back into the water and slowly sank below. Liza Tower Hill was dead, or so the legend goes.

To this day, it is said that the Allyn House is haunted by the spirit of Liza. The house lays claim to being the eighth oldest on Cape Cod, built in the late 1600s and for many years occupied by one of the Cape's most well-to-do families, the Allyns.

Present owners Jack and Lore Garner, who bought the property in 1995, invited me into this historic home one night for a private tour. All rooms in the original part of the house surround a central chimney. The honey-colored, wide pine floors gently tilt and softly creak, revealing their age. In the Keeping Room, where Colonial families spent most of their time in the winter months, there is a massive hearth and beehive oven. Today the Keeping Room serves as the Garner's dining room. Just off the kitchen, there is a small bathroom. This tiny room, warmed by the hearth, was formerly used as the Borning Room; and as the name indicates, it was the room where babies were often delivered. The sick and dying were also comforted there. Despite various alterations, this charming saltbox looks very much as it did back when the Allyns owned the house.

At one point, the Allyn family hired one of Liza's daughters, Lydia, as a servant. Unfortunately for the Allyns, they did not treat her very well. When Liza heard about the mistreatments she cast a spell on the house. Suddenly, a strange cat appeared and eerie happenings began to transpire. Mysterious lights were seen throughout the house. Footsteps and strange knocking noises were heard. Furniture was found broken, dishes were smashed and fresh milk soured. Some family members heard skirts swooshing by and reported feeling a terrible, dark presence.

Throughout the years the hauntings have persisted. Although some former owners have not reported ghostly activity, the present owners have a tale to tell. A man who once lived across the street told Lore Garner that he witnessed the door leading to the staircase in the Keeping Room open and close by itself. When Lore's granddaughter came for a visit one time, she saw the door leading from the kitchen to the Keeping Room open and close by itself. Mysterious voices have also been known to echo throughout the house. Lore claims she has heard the voice of a person speaking, or sometimes it will sound as if several people are having a conversation. Just recently, she heard the voice of a woman clearly say the word, "Wait." One time while Jack Garner was in the barn beside the house he began to hear the voices of children giggling and conversing. When he dashed outside, not a child was to be found. Jack has also heard strange noises at night, such as loud banging coming from outside. Both the Garners seem to just take these encounters in stride and sometimes even talk to the spirits, offering friendly hellos and saying, "Let's be friends."

It should be noted that historical records indicate that Liza Tower Hill was a member in full communion of the East Church in Barnstable; and upon her death in 1790, she was honored by her pastor as an exemplary and pious worshiper.

Her ashes are buried in the East Church graveyard.

The Haunted Barn

The historic Bacon Barn, situated in Barnstable Village, is currently owned by Pat and Jack Coffey. I interviewed Pat on a dark and stormy night. Here is what she said:

When we began looking for a house on the Cape, this one was the first house the realtor showed us. I didn't like the exterior of the home, nor did I like the location; but as soon as I walked through the front door a warmth came over me. I knew this was my house. I hadn't even met the owners, but I was already picturing where I was going to place my furniture.

The house, which was once a barn and used primarily to house cows, was part of the Bacon Farm and owned by the Bacon family in the 1800s. Daniel C. Bacon, a sea captain, built his main house next door.

We bought the house in the month of January. I drove down to visit with my daughter and her children, but for some reason the house just didn't feel the same to me. The first thing I thought to myself was, "Did I make a mistake in buying this house?"

We moved into the house in May. We didn't have any of our furniture with us. It wasn't going to be delivered until June. Fortunately, the previous owners left the bedroom furniture for us.

I remember one afternoon my husband Jack was upstairs in the loft hooking up speakers to the stereo, and I was in the kitchen. All of a sudden, I heard, "Click. Click. Click." It was the sound of heels coming down the stairs and across the floor. I thought to myself, "I wonder what that is?" But there was nobody there. I really didn't think too much of it and soon forgot about it. That night Jack and I went out for dinner at the Mattakeese Restaurant. It was a very foggy and spooky night. While we were sitting in the restaurant, Jack said to me, "Did you hear footsteps this afternoon?" I said to him, "Yes, I did, but let's discuss it in the morning."

Well, the next morning it was sunny and bright and Jack questioned me again about the footsteps. He said, "I thought it was you." And I said, "I thought it was you."

Before I left for the week I hung my candle sconces on the wall. When I returned Friday night, I noticed the sconces on the left were on the floor with the candles intact. It was like someone had taken them down and gently placed them on the floor. In fact, the hook was still on the wall. This happened more than once.

I said to Jack, "I don't think she likes where I put these sconces," referring to the spirit who I assumed was a woman because of the sound of heels. Well, Jack was not accepting any of this. He kept saying, "That stuff isn't true!" A friend of mine who knows a lot about art told me to move the sconces over about three inches, and to this day the sconces have never come off the wall again.

There were other little things that used to happen as well. For instance, I would put something in a certain place and if I wasn't sure if it looked right, I would often come back and find it askew. I would straighten whatever it was and leave the room, only to come back and find it askew again. I also began to see this white haze whenever I walked up the staircase to the second floor. The haze began at the front bedroom and swept across to the fireplace, just like a fog. Then it would disappear as if someone had sucked it up with a vacuum. Others who have visited the house for the first time have also witnessed this haze.

That first summer was brutally hot. I believe it was the month of July, when the children were down visiting. I was off Cape and didn't get home until five. When I walked in, there was no one home. The kitchen was an absolute mess. There were dishes piled everywhere, and I'm kind of a neatnik. I began to put the dishes into the dishwasher, when suddenly I began to feel a presence. I turned around and standing on the rug in the hallway was a woman. She was very petite with beautiful gray hair. She wore a long black dress, but had no face. She was standing there and then just disappeared.

My daughter and I have also seen a woman with long black hair sitting on the coffee table in the living room. She began to appear right after we bought the table, a couple of years after we moved in. She would always sit facing the fireplace, but you couldn't see her reflection in the glass doors on the fireplace. I believe it has been three years since we have seen her.

When the children first began visiting, I noticed how active the house became just after they would leave. I used to brace myself because I knew what was about to happen. All of the doors on the second floor would open and slam shut. "Bang! Bang! Bang!" In my granddaughter's room, who was three years old at the time, we had a very strange experience. About four o'clock in the morning, my daughter, who was sleeping in another bedroom, began to hear over the baby monitor, "Mommy! Mommy! Mommy!" She dashed into my granddaughter's room and upon entering saw what she described as a little boy wearing a baseball uniform, although I think he was probably wearing knickers. She said the little boy was bending over looking at all the Beanie Babies that my granddaughter sleeps with, and then he just disappeared. My granddaughter remained fast asleep. *My daughter also told me that one morning she heard my granddaughter laughing and playing in her room. She said she walked into the room and asked her whom she was playing with. My granddaughter replied, "The lady." My daughter asked if she was scared, and she replied, "No, she's funny. She makes me laugh."*

One afternoon Jack and I decided to take the grandchildren on the Cape Cod train because my daughter wasn't feeling well and really needed to get some rest. When we returned she said she barely got any sleep because a child's voice kept calling out to her, "Mommy! Mommy!" and then she found herself staring at the little boy, once again.

If that wasn't enough, we even have a ghost cat that floats around the house. My daughter was the first one to experience this ghost cat. She said that while putting the kids in the tub in the front bedroom, she began to hear what sounded like a cat dashing around, and the dust ruffles on the bed began to move. When she mentioned this to me, I honestly thought it was her cat; but one night we were sitting in the kitchen and we heard this thud. We both looked up and there was this huge, white Angora cat that jumped from the window ledge to the countertop and then just vanished.

I have to tell you that I find it very strange that a house that was primarily used as a dairy farm in the 1800s and virtually uninhabited by people until 1971 would have so many spirits living here!

11 Ghosts

There are few structures on Cape Cod that have a more haunted reputation than the Barnstable House on Old Kings Highway. For years I have driven by this stately Colonial house, with its massive black and white chimney, almost completely oblivious to its very existence. Thankfully, I now know much more. My drive by will certainly never be the same.

The Barnstable House was originally framed in Scituate, Massachusetts. It was then shipped to Barnstable and constructed by James Paine in 1716. Paine's grandson, Robert Treat Paine, was a signer of the Declaration of Independence. The estate was eventually purchased by a man named Edmund Hawes. On October 1, 1776,

Elisha Doane bought the home from Hawes and paid for it in Continental currency, which had just become worthless, thanks to the American Revolution. Hawes was so distraught he committed suicide by hanging himself from a tree on the property.

In 1799 a doctor named Samuel Savage became the new owner. Savage retained ownership until his death when it was inherited by his daughter Hope Savage Shaw, who was the second wife of Chief Justice Lemuel Shaw. The house was then sold to Abner Davis in 1832. Davis died in 1839, and the house was inherited by his wife Nancy and then passed on to her son, Adolphas, who was a Boston ship owner. During this time the house was occupied by a supposedly unfriendly sea captain named John Grey.

In the 1900s the home was converted into an inn and restaurant. It was owned by a number of different people and operated under many different names, including the 1716 House, Old Jail House, The Sign of the Blue Lantern, Andrea Doria Inn, Captain Grey's and finally the Barnstable House. During the 1980s, it was converted into an office building managed by Bob and Marie Scales, owners of Clark Engineered Products.

Marie gave me a private tour of this magnificent building, which has been impeccably restored, with many of the original features still intact.

As I previously mentioned, the Barnstable House has quite a haunted reputation. A séance was once performed here, and a psychic claimed eleven different entities roam the house. Probably the most famous sighting involved four fire fighters back in the 1970s. At approximately 3:00 A.M. the Barnstable Fire Department received a call for help from the Barnstable House. Two fire trucks were immediately dispatched to the scene. Upon arrival the fire fighters caught a glimpse of a woman in one of the upstairs windows. Several fire fighters rushed up to save her but could not find a trace of the woman. After they cleared the smoke, several fire fighters saw the same woman, now outside and hovering two feet above the snow. She was described as having long blonde hair and wearing a long white dress. The firemen said she wore a sad expression and wondered around the property. It was said that she disappeared before the fire fighters could reach her.

One person who had owned the house when it was an inn and restaurant told a story that involved high school students who were trying to photograph ghosts with infrared film at night. Apparently while inside the house, the students were not well-behaved and made a racket upstairs. The owner was in a downstairs bedroom trying to sleep when suddenly she was awakened by a bright light. A massive fire had ignited by itself in the fireplace. The owner believed the spirits did not like the students wandering the house and when she asked them to be quiet, the flames suddenly extinguished.

Another incident involved a young boy and his mother who were guests of the inn. The boy was said to have drawn pictures of the house with flames and ghosts coming out of the windows. He was quoted saying, "See what the ghosts did to the house? They're silly ghosts. They're terrible ghosts." The owner said she got an uneasy feeling and asked the boy not to say that anymore. After the boy went to bed that night, the owner walked downstairs, and to her amazement found an old candle chandelier burning brightly. She blew out the candles and then returned shortly thereafter only to find them relit.

There is another presence that is thought to reside in the dark damp cellar. This spirit has been identified as the cantankerous Captain Grey. He is known as the "door slammer."

A spirit of a young girl named Lucy is also thought to reside here. It was said that she drowned in a stream that ran under the house. A rocking chair that now sits beside the fireplace in the main lobby has been seen rocking by itself on occasion. The rocking chair spirit is thought to be Lucy's mother, patiently rocking in the chair, waiting for her daughter's return.

The woman sighted by the fire fighters has been identified by some mediums as Martha. It is not known exactly why her spirit remains, but some have said she is simply waiting. To this day there are people who refuse to work in the Barnstable House alone.

The Chair Man

LAMB AND LION INN

T ucked away on Old Kings Highway just west of Barnstable Village lies a sprawling 18th century inn, known as the Lamb and Lion.

The main part of the inn was constructed in 1740. The Keeping Room next to the dining room is cozy and comfortable. If the weather is less than ideal, it's a perfect place for reading or conversation. The inn features no less than 10 guestrooms ranging from simple and charming to rather extravagant. A room known as the Lion's Den features a private staircase, fireplace, kitchen and private bath. The Lamb's Retreat, once horse stables, is now a two-bedroom cottage with an attached kitchen, living room and private bath, overlooking flower gardens and woods. The Innkeeper's Pride is another gem featuring a fireplace, kitchen, bath with sunken tub and a private deck. The largest accommodation is a converted barn built in 1740 with three lofts, one bath, living room, kitchen and barbecue deck. The inn also harbors an outdoor swimming pool.

Innkeeper Alice Pitcher, originally from Nantucket, is a gracious host with a warm inner glow. When she purchased the Lamb and Lion from its previous owner, he mentioned that he rarely rented out the barn. When asked why, he commented that there were a lot of strange noises and other problems related to the barn. Alice suggested that the barn might in fact have a ghost, and he did not disagree.

Alice is by no means a stranger to ghosts. We chatted about an inn she previously owned in upper New York state that was haunted by a ghost named Ebenezer. Ebenezer was not a very well-behaved ghost. He was always turning on water faucets and crashing and banging around.

With experience on her side, Alice asked the former owner to go into more detail about the problems in the barn. Other than the noises, he mentioned that he could never keep the door to the barn closed. Alice knew she wanted to renovate the barn for rental purposes. If there were a ghost, she figured she would have to make her peace with it. Sometime after renovations were completed, she remembered walking into the barn around dusk to turn the lights on for arriving guests. She stepped into the room and immediately felt as if there were someone in the room with her. She was just about to turn the light on when she saw a huge man with a pointy beard and muddy boots wearing a vest with pockets. The man was sitting in a chair beneath the stairs and looking out the window. She abruptly switched the light on to get a better look, but the man vanished. Alice ran back over to the main house and told her partner of the incident. As she was describing the man who was sitting in the chair, her partner stopped her and said, "Chair, what chair are you talking about? There isn't a chair under the stairs!"

Now Alice was starting to believe that maybe neither the chair nor the man had really been there. They both ran back to the barn, but the chair was still under the stairs. Apparently, Alice's brother had put an old rickety chair in the basement after trying unsuccessfully to sell it in a tag sale. How it made it to the barn remains a mystery to this day. Alice said she wasn't frightened by the man, and that he didn't seem to acknowledge her presence. He just sat gazing out the window with an expression on his face that made her think he was contemplating something.

Before the barn was completely renovated, Alice's brother frequently stayed there during the winter months. From time to time, he clearly remembered hearing a man sigh. Alice decided to leave the old chair under the stairs and is quick to admit that sometimes it is found facing different directions.

Maybe it's just the guests moving the chair around, or maybe, just maybe, it's something else.

LAMB AND LION INN
BARNSTABLE, MASSACHUSETTS
508-362-6823

Ghost Machine

Shown here is wallpaper made up of pages from 19th-century publications.

I n the words of an anonymous man from Yarmouth Port:

The Captain Oliver Matthews House was built in 1835 and is one of a large number of historic houses in Yarmouth Port.

In the 1970s, my mother was down visiting her sister in Dennis. She just happened to see this house for sale and got really impulsive. I said, "Mom, go for it!" At the time we were living in Lexington. Father had died and my mother wanted to be closer to her sister. Besides, it was a lovely old house with a lot of charm and hadn't been modified very much. The house had a lot of unique features. In the kitchen, for example, there is a hot water heater that you have to light a fire underneath in order to get hot water. In the attic, there is this really marvelous room, which is entirely papered with magazines dating back to the 1800s.

We moved into the house in 1971. We never had any kind of ghostly occurrence until around 1976 or so, when my mother and some of her friends were staying there. At one point they looked at each other and said, "Who put the coffee on?" There was this distinct aroma of coffee circulating around the house, but of course, no one had made any coffee. That was the first unusual incident. Around that time, something rather strange began to happen. Women visiting the house would mysteriously lose one of their earrings. Not terribly ghostly, I know, but nevertheless another strange, unexplainable occurrence.

In 1980 my mother passed away but my wife and I kept the house as a summer residence. Since there are only the two of us and we didn't get down to the home that often, we loaned it out to friends and family. That winter we hadn't gotten the heat fixed, but my friend John decided to stay there anyway. He kept himself warm by lighting all of the fireplaces in the house. John was a handy guy and kept a bunch of tools in the house. He began to notice that some of them had disappeared. John searched high and low, but the tools were gone. He started to get angry and said in a loud voice, "All right, look, these are not earrings. Give me my tools back!" He went into the cellar for one last look, came back upstairs, and there were the tools, sitting on the kitchen table.

A year later, some members of my wife's family were staying in the house. There were some young children there as well, and one of them walked into the kitchen and said, "Mom, who's the sad man and the lady in pink?" Mom, of course, got very upset and bailed out of the house. That was the very first recorded sighting in the house. The second sighting happened a few years later. Another child reported seeing a sad-looking man, and a lady in pink as well. After the second sighting, we all came to the conclusion that it must have been the original occupants, Phoebe and Oliver, who were haunting the house.

Another unusual experience happened to friends of mine that were residing in the house for a period of time. Apparently one of them could not find the linen closet and was getting very upset. They went out for a while, and when they returned, the door to the linen closet was wide open and a towel was on the floor.

In my opinion, the ultimate ghost story happened to a woman I worked with and her brother who I let use the house. The woman told me that while they were staying there, her brother teased her children. He told them that Phoebe was a mean ghost and was going to get them during the night. She said she tried to talk him out of telling scary stories to the kids, but he wouldn't listen. Her brother was residing in one of the upstairs bedrooms. At about 2:00 A.M., he had to go to the bathroom. He got out of bed and attempted to open the bedroom door, but the door would not open. He was locked in his room.

She said he really flipped out, yelling, "Let me out! Let me out!" But the door would not budge. Eventually he gave up and fell back to sleep. When he awoke the next morning the bedroom door was wide open.

My friend John, the one who had the experience with the missing tools, seems to have some ghostly sensitivity. He claims to have seen a ghost in the town of Marblehead and another one in Rangeley, Maine. Although he has never had a sighting at my house, he knew there were spirits here. Well, both of use decided it was time to break out the Ouija board. The Ouija board told us there are, in fact, four ghosts in the house: Phoebe and Oliver, one ghost that was illiterate and could not identify itself through the Ouija board, and another ghost named Ellen. Apparently Ellen is the ghost that takes the earrings, although we could never figure out why.

One day I decided to do some research on the house. I asked my next-door neighbor for some help. His family was quite connected with the area. In fact, his aunt had even owned my house for a period of time. I asked him if he knew anything about a person named Ellen in connection with my house. He asked his family and was told that a distant relative from England who was named Ellen once stayed there for two winters. They said she was really weird.

Now, have you ever heard of a ghost that decided to return transatlantic? I guess she decided that she didn't want to be a ghost in England and managed to hitchhike passage over here, so she could hang out at the Matthews house!

Now, I want to show you something that John found in a Popular Mechanics *magazine. After seeing this device, I decided to try to make one. It is allegedly a ghost detector. It detects very subtle changes in electromagnetic fields. The device is incredibly sensitive, and when it detects something, it makes a tapping noise. We tested the ghost detector out in a notoriously haunted place off-Cape. We were very disappointed; no ghostly detection. We then tried it out at my house in Yarmouth Port. In the room wallpapered with old magazines dating back to the 1800s, the detector began to sound off, signaling ghostly activity.*

Sometime after that, I was doing some work on the house by myself. I brought the ghost machine with me and set it down in the hallway. I said aloud, "If you like the work I'm doing, set off the machine." Suddenly the machine sounded off. I then said, "Ok, turn it off," but this time there was no response.

Ghostly Guestbook

THE COLONIAL HOUSE INN

lovely home was constructed by the Josiah Ryder family back in the 1730s on the Old Kings Highway in Yarmouth Port. The original structure was a two-story, federal-style, hip-roof building. The house was eventually purchased by Joseph Eldridge and became known as the Eldridge house for the next century.

In the 1820s another house was floated over from Nantucket and placed on a foundation at the rear of the building. In the 1860s,

Dr. Azariah Eldridge took ownership of the house. He moved the Nantucket house and added it to the main structure. Dr. Eldridge also added the third floor, with its mansard roof and Doric portico that give the place such a distinct Victorian look.

By 1979 the mansion had been abandoned and was sorely in need of repair. The house had no electricity, no plumbing and no heat. The windows were boarded up and the ceilings were collapsing due to extensive water damage. The building was literally a wreck. But after two years of renovations, Mac Perna had successfully transformed this once private summer residence into a thriving dining and lodging establishment, the renowned Colonial House Inn. In 1988 it was placed on the National Register of Historic Places.

The main building boasts three dining rooms: the Oak Room, the Colonial Room and a glass-enclosed veranda known as the Common. The comfortable lounge, with a well-stocked bar, is a cozy place where patrons can sip cocktails by the glow of a warm fire on raw winter nights.

Guestrooms in the main house, as well as in the carriage house, are clean and comfortable with period antique furnishings, and the inn also features a pretty garden area surrounded by a lush, sprawling lawn where wedding vows are often heard, followed by kissing and applause. According to Mac, these spiritual unions are the only spiritual activities at the Inn. "If I should ever see a ghost around here, I would either put a hammer in his hand or give him a bill for staying here," said Mac.

A bit of a skeptic, Mac has never personally experienced any type of paranormal activity for as long as he has owned the inn. However, just because Mac hasn't witnessed any unusual happenings does not mean the inn is void of ghostly energy. These ghostly inhabitants may be keeping their distance from Mac, but not from his guests.

Mac keeps a record of his guest's haunted experiences, what could be described as a "ghostly guestbook," if you will. But he is quick to point out that he does not encourage this sort of thing. He feels that if he makes a statement about what happens in a given room in a given time of year, then it could stay embedded in some-one's subconscious, causing them to imagine something. Instead, if a guest happens to ask, Mac will relate the specific incidences, but never the rooms in which they have occurred. That way he knows the experiences are as credible as possible. That being said, the stories Mac has collected for over twenty years have shown a remarkable sameness. I'm sorry I can't tell you what rooms are the most active, because Mac wouldn't tell me either. I can relate some of the tales, however.

Mac says there is one room where people have frequently reported hearing a baby cry or children yelling. Years ago when the mansion was in its heyday, that very room was occupied by a child who tragically died of a disease. The door has the child's name on it, but since all of the guestrooms are named after former residents, this really isn't much of a clue.

In another room, Mac consistently hears about a family rocker that seems to move across the room by itself. Guests have reported sitting in the chair in a particular place in the room, but when they awake in the morning the chair not only has been moved, but it usually ends up directly facing a wall that used to have a window. Mac says he even tried putting different rocking chairs in that room to see if the reports would change, but all the rockers seem to be positioned mysteriously facing the wall in the morning. Some people have reported a distinct presence when they have walked by this room, as well as the child's room, which are both located in the main building.

In the carriage house, reports of a young man crying and the sounds of horses have surfaced. Mac says the only guests that have reported hearing the young man are guests that have resided in one particular room in the carriage house. That room is where the stable boys used to reside. The room where the sounds of horses are occasionally heard was in fact the old horse stables.

Over the years, there have been other reports of strange happenings as well, but they seem to be less consistent. I had the good fortune of interviewing a librarian who is employed at the Dennis Public Library. She and her husband have had some strange experiences while staying at the Colonial House Inn. Here is her story:

It was probably 18 or 20 years ago. My husband thought I was waking him in the middle of the night, only to realize that I was sleeping on the opposite side of the bed. He felt someone tapping him on the shoulder, and when he looked up he saw a thin, transparent figure of a woman dressed in 1800s clothing and wearing a bonnet.

A year or two after that, in another room in the middle of the night, I felt pressure on my back. I was so scared, I couldn't even call out to my husband! I managed to get the courage to roll over, and when I did, I saw a shadowy figure that was very low to the ground. Then it just vanished out of the room!

THE COLONIAL HOUSE INN
YARMOUTH PORT, MA
508-362-4348
800-999-3416

A Suicidal Ghost

SCARGO CAFE

hen I heard that there were ghost stories surrounding one of my favorite restaurants, I jumped into my car and sped down 6A towards Dennis. The Scargo Cafe offers great food, wonderful service and has always been a favorite among locals and tourists alike.

This lovely building was built after the Civil War by Luther Hall in 1868. Luther was born on November 5, 1842 in Dennis,

Massachusetts, the son of Thomas and Hepsy Hall. A Civil War veteran, Luther's discharge papers are kept in the Dennis Historical Society Library. After serving his enlistment period, he was discharged at 19 years of age from Captain John Kent's Company E, 5th Regiment of Massachusetts volunteers. At the time of enrollment he was a clerk. After his discharge, he reenlisted for an additional 100 days. Later, he was commissioned a Captain of Militia by Governor Andrews. When Luther returned home, he sought employment as a clerk in Howes Chapman's store, located where the Mobil station currently stands next door to the restaurant on Route 6A. He later took possession of the property where the Scargo Cafe is presently located, and in 1868 he built his home there. The following year he married his boss's daughter, Minerva. In time, Luther took over Chapman's store and operated it until 1885. He also served as the village Postmaster until 1886. When Luther retired from the shop, he went into the cranberry business. He next became 'agent in charge' of the Nobscussett Hotel and eventually the Superintendent of the Dennis school system. He died on April 29, 1800 at the age of 58.

Cafe owner Peter Troutman says unusual occurrences have taken place here on occasion, and some have thought that the ghost of Luther Hall has been responsible. Peter purchased the property in the 1980s. There were previously five restaurants that operated on the site. Prior to that, the house had been occupied by a Dennis tax collector.

In the early years of the Scargo Cafe, Peter remembers a frightening presence that used to occupy the second floor. Originally bedrooms, the second floor now serves as an office and storage space. According to Peter, this presence gave the wait staff a very creepy feeling whenever they went upstairs, particularly at night. Peter himself confessed that he hated to work alone on the second floor and would get strange chills when darkness fell. One of the bedrooms had been set aside as a changing room for the wait staff. However, I was told the staff would often run upstairs, get their clothes, dash downstairs and change in the public restrooms, as none of them wanted to be upstairs any longer than was absolutely necessary.

One particular waiter had a chilling experience one evening while alone upstairs. During a large gathering at the restaurant, he ran upstairs to get a highchair out of the storage room. Before he walked back downstairs, he set the highchair down and was about to get something else when suddenly he felt as if unseen hands were trying to push him down the stairs. Others have reported feeling as if someone was touching them on the neck while on the second floor.

Peter informed me these strange happenings occurred regularly from 1987 until 1990, when all paranormal activity abruptly ceased. Peter theorizes that the cessation of activity was related to a waitress who worked seasonally at the restaurant. After the summer of 1990, this waitress had stopped by the restaurant to say her good-byes before returning to school. Her friend, who was still working at the restaurant, received a phone call from her shortly after she arrived back at school. She mentioned that while she was driving away from the restaurant, down the Mid-Cape Highway, she felt the presence of the ghost in the car with her. As she was driving across the canal bridge the presence suddenly vanished from her car as if it had jumped from the bridge to its death. As if a ghost could do such a thing! Certainly, this waitress felt as if it were a kind of ghostly suicide.

The staff might not have taken this report seriously, except for the fact that the presence was not felt again.

SCARGO CAFE
DENNIS, MASSACHUSETTS
508-385-8200

A Pat on the Rump

THE DENNIS INN

The setting is one of tranquility: a sprawling, weather-shingled Colonial set on spacious grounds, surrounded by manicured shrubs and blooming, springtime flowers.

The Dennis Inn dates back to 1928 when it was built as a private summer home. In 1947 it became an inn and restaurant. The present owners, Linda Garland and Sebastian Falcone, originally operated the business as an inn and restaurant. They began specializing in special events, and over time they enjoyed this part of the business so much that they slowly phased out everything else and now focus on weddings and other private functions.

After a brief tour I said to Sebastian, "I understand your inn has a ghost." Sebastian replied, "You say ghost, we just use that word because we don't know how else to label this."

Sebastian said when he first purchased the inn, odd little occurrences began to happen. At first he kept it to himself until his staff began mentioning funny little things that they, too, were experiencing. That's when everyone began sharing their stories. They all came to the realization they might be sharing the inn with a ghost.

Sebastian said that a magazine once did an article about their ghost. After receiving many letters from people inquiring about the ghost, he received a startling phone call. The woman started by saying, "I just want you to know I'm not a nut. In fact my niece lives right next to you. I have a story I think you might be interested in."

The woman went on to say that she used to summer at the inn (when it was still a private home) back in the 1940s. Apparently, her sister's husband was a pilot during World War II. He was shot down, captured and imprisoned in Germany. One day out of the blue, the family maid said, "Your husband is out of prison." The woman made an inquiry at the Veterans Administration about her husband's release. No one had any information about his status. Two and a half days later the Veterans Administration called the house. They had just received word that her husband had escaped from the German prison camp. It seemed that the maid was clairvoyant. After reading the article in the magazine, this woman had called the Dennis Inn to tell them she believed that it was the maid's ghost haunting the inn.

I asked Sebastian to go into some detail about the ghost. He began by saying that every so often when he climbs into bed at night, he feels the other side of the bed go down as if someone has just joined him. Apparently, this began happening from day one and still continues.

Sebastian recalled when Linda's mother was out in the yard one day cutting flowers. She took her gloves off, put her scissors on the gloves and went in for a little break. When she returned to the yard, the scissors were nowhere to be found. About a year later Sebastian needed an end table that was stored in the attic. When he picked up the table, he heard something sliding in the drawer. He put the table down and opened the drawer. Incredibly, inside were the scissors Linda's mother had lost a year previously.

Sebastian's son had a little run-in with the ghost as well. Wanting to move to the Cape, his son had driven down one evening for a job interview the next morning. While he was sleeping, he was awakened by a cold draft. He climbed out of bed, closed the window and went back to sleep. Again he was awakened by a cold draft. The window he had closed was now wide open. His son was so frightened that he left in the middle of the night.

The inn once employed a bartender who used to scoff at the notion of the place harboring a ghost. Sebastian said he was a handsome bodybuilder with a big ego to boot. One evening after the bar had closed the bartender was in the wine cellar stocking up for the next day. While bending over to grab a bottle, he felt a pat on his rump. Thinking it was a waitress, he quickly straightened up and turned around. He was astonished to find himself completely alone.

He walked out of the wine cellar with eyes as big as saucers. He was now a believer. He even went so far as to name the ghost. He called her Lillian after his stepmother, whom he despised.

THE DENNIS INN
DENNIS, MASSACHUSETTS
508-385-6571

Push!

OLD YARMOUTH INN

I can't remember how many times I've driven by the Old Yarmouth Inn in Yarmouth Port over the years, or why I've never stopped by. I was recently informed the inn had just changed hands and decided to drop in one Saturday evening to sample their fare.

If it's superb, creative cuisine, a cozy atmosphere, and a courteous staff you've been searching for, this inn is a must! Listed in the National Register of Historical Places, the Old Yarmouth Inn is one of the oldest inns on Cape Cod. It was built in 1696 and served as a stagecoach stop for many years. An original guestbook dating from 1869 is on display for the guests' enjoyment.

Sheila FitzGerald and her husband Arpad Voros purchased the inn in 1996. Knowing how old the inn was I simply had to ask if they had a ghost. They were told by the previous owners that the inn was haunted. Arpad said they really didn't pay much attention to their warning and more or less brushed it off. That was then. Rest assured, Arpad and Sheila are now believers! They both began sharing some of their experiences with me one night by the fire.

Sheila stated that the first person to have a run-in with their ghost was her sister, Maureen. It was early one morning when Maureen came downstairs to make a cup of coffee. As she was about to enter the dark kitchen, she began to hear noises. Frightened that someone might be in the kitchen, she threw open the door, turned on the light and found the bread mixer operating by itself.

One evening after hours, Arpad, Sheila and Maureen were all relaxing in the tavern, when suddenly they began to hear a groaning, howling sound coming from inside the wall. At that point the walls and windows began shaking and rattling. Sheila said it was almost indescribable; they had never experienced anything like it.

The ghost also seems to play little tricks including plucking wineglasses off the rack and sending them crashing to the ground. Arpad also recalls seeing an ashtray jump off the top of a pile and slide down the entire length of the bar by itself.

I forgot to mention something. The inn rents out four of its rooms to guests, which brings us to our final story. One morning a guest awoke and walked downstairs to get a freshly brewed cup of coffee. The coffee is always kept in the kitchen, and the guests are asked to help themselves. When the guest arrived at the kitchen door, she was a little confused about which door to enter. Restaurants usually have two doors, one for exiting the kitchen and one for entering. Not being familiar with restaurant doors, she wondered which door to enter and why the doors didn't have handles. Suddenly, from nowhere a disembodied voice from beyond uttered, "Push!"

OLD YARMOUTH INN
YARMOUTH PORT, MASSACHUSETTS
508-362-9962

The
LOWER
CAPE

Antique Horror

I n the words of an anonymous woman from Brewster:

This started back in the summer of 1990. My mom and I went to Eldred's Auction House [on Route 6A in Dennis] for the Americana Auction. We first previewed all the pieces, and sitting there was this Bible box. The tag said, "Early 1700s, Pennsylvania." The box was about 14 inches by 10 inches, and it was oak with these amazing, medieval-like hinges. It really looked like it should have been in a museum, just gorgeous. Eventually, it came up for auction, and there were these two other people and myself bidding on it. Well, I hung in there and I got it. I was even congratulated by the two other bidders. We brought the box home [to Brewster], and of course my mom was very excited. She thought it was a great piece.

Shortly after, I took my two golden retrievers for a swim at the park. I can remember not feeling very well. When I was in the water, my stomach was very unsettled.

About two weeks later, strange little things began to happen around the house. Fire alarms began to go off, and one painting kept falling off the wall. I was still not feeling very well. They were just little things, and I really didn't pay too much attention to them.

It was probably about three weeks after I got the box, I went over to my friend's house who owns an antique shop. When I was walking through the shop, I noticed this one-of-a kind dressmaker's doll from the 1700s. The doll was full-figured from the waist up with movable joints. She was like a modern-day mannequin. They would dress her up to show what the latest styles would have been back in that time period. I ended up buying it, although I'm not really sure

117

why. I guess it was because it was old and one of a kind. I don't really even like dolls.

That night I got home very late and put the doll by the entertainment center. The Bible box was in the Keeping Room. I walked upstairs and went to bed. In the middle of the night, I woke up to a scratching sound in the wall that was becoming more and more intense. About a month prior to that, we had bees that had burrowed into the windowsills. I tried to spray most of them, but I thought that maybe some of the bees had spread into the walls. I did my best to fall back to sleep, but I kept waking up to that noise.

The next day, I had completely forgotten about the strange noises. That night I went to bed late again. During the night, I awoke to this popping sound coming through the wall. I didn't pay too much attention to it. I thought perhaps it was something coming from outside. About fifteen minutes later, I heard this bang up against the wall. Now I'm thinking, "All right, now what?" Fifteen minutes later, it became louder and louder. Now all through the night, I'm hearing this banging sound. Well, when things like that start to happen, you don't start thinking about ghosts; you start thinking logically, like maybe it was the pipes or a squirrel.

From 1:00 AM to 8:00 AM this sound continued. I noticed it seemed to be coming from downstairs and every once in a while, the sound would be so loud that my bed would vibrate. I went through every logical explanation I could think of. By 8:00 AM, I had come to the conclusion that there must be something in the house that I don't know about. Something that is not of this world. That morning I went over to my neighbor to borrow something. Before I left, I said to her, "You don't happen to believe in ghosts do you?" She asked why, and I said there's something going on in my house, and I proceeded to tell her about the noises. She said, "Oh, I know a friend that had a ghost in her house. You have to get in touch with this woman who is a medium. I will get you her name. That doesn't sound like your house at all."

Well, sure enough, the noises started up again. This time, it sounded like fireworks in the distance, then the popping noises, and eventually the intense banging started. It was almost like someone was taking a ball and whipping it up against the wall. Then it sounded like the ball bouncing back. It often sounded as if the ball were hitting different spots in the room. Once in a while, it would sound as if it were bouncing off the ceiling, causing my bed to shake.

The next morning at about 8:00 AM the noises stopped. It seemed that when the sun rose to a certain point in the sky, everything would suddenly stop. I just kept thinking to myself, "What is going on?" The only thing I had brought into the house was a Bible box and a doll. Those were the only two things that were new to the house. That morning, my neighbor came over with the phone number of the medium. She said, "You really have to call her." That night at about 9:00 PM, I called her and told her that something was going on in my house and proceeded to tell her about the noises. The medium said to me, "You have a black Windsor rocker in your house, don't you?" I said, "Yes I do." She said, "Well, he's sitting in it."

I said, "Who is sitting in it?"

She replied, "The minister. There is a minister in your house, and he's mad because he's in a Catholic household. Don't worry, he's not there to harm you, but if you want me to come over, I will."

I told her to come over, particularly because I wasn't getting any sleep.

The next night the medium came over at 7:00 PM. She pulled into the driveway and told me she wanted to walk my property line. We began to walk along the side of the house, and eventually she walked up to the main part of the house. She turned her head very quickly to look in the window and then turned away. She then turned again and looked back into the window; she looked away and began walking the property again. She proceeded to tell me that she really doesn't like to do this; she called it "ghost busting." She said it was time for her to see the two items.

By now, I had the doll and the Bible box outside at the end of the property underneath a steel metal bin. She wanted to go to the north side of the property for the ritual she was about to perform. The medium pulled out a blanket and picked up the doll and examined it. "No," she said, " this isn't it." Then she picked up the Bible box and said, "This is it. His name is Isaac, and he is a minister of the fire-and-brimstone school." That school meant if you didn't do what the minister said you would be damned and go to hell. She also said that he was a child molester and not a very nice person. Apparently he would entice the children with toys to come into his house, and this doll was upsetting him because it reminded him of his evil ways. She said that not only did he molest the children, but also the women of the parish. She went on to say that he thinks he's come home again, not because of the size of the house but because of how the house is situated, being surrounded by trees and set back by itself. She told me he was in my house with his black coat and round hat, waiting for us. I began to think to myself, "I don't want anything to do with this or the house right now."

The medium began to perform the ceremony. She started to burn sage and a couple of other things before we walked into the house. When it was time to go inside, we walked through the front door, and she immediately looked into the room to the right and said, "No, he's not here." Then we went around through the hallway into the Keeping Room. She took out a statue of the Virgin Mary and a Bible. She said to me, "I want you to open up the Bible to whatever passage you come to and read it."

I opened the Bible to a passage where Jesus had died and three days later He came back again, and His apostles thought He was a ghost. I couldn't believe I had opened to that passage. Well, I finished reading and she did some type of blessing, and then she said, "He's gone."

I said, "What do you mean he's gone?"

She said, "He's going up the street right now. He thinks that he has another ministry to go to. Don't worry, he's gone. Just relax, he's not going to bother you anymore. If you're in trouble at any time your Guardian Angel is there to protect you. Light a candle and pray to her."

The medium left at about nine o'clock that night. My neighbor called and asked what had happened. I said, "Everything is fine. She got rid of him, and I'm finally going to get a good night's sleep." I went up to my bedroom, put on the TV and went to sleep. That night the noises returned, and they were more intense than ever. I was so upset I actually ran to the bathroom and got sick. I kept thinking, "What is happening? He's supposed to be gone! I can't believe this!"

I crawled back into bed. The noises were so loud that the entire bed was shaking. I thought the only thing I could do was what she had told me – pray to my Guardian Angel. I crept out of bed very quietly, lit a candle and began to pray. The noises suddenly stopped. I crept back into bed, pulled the covers up and bang! The noises started back up. I did this three times that night. Every time I lit the candle and prayed the noises would stop, but when I climbed into bed the noises would start again.

I called the medium the next night and told her the noises were back and now they're worse than ever. She said, "Well he's not there. It's not him. I don't know if you've disturbed something else that's been brought into your house, but it's not him."

Now I'm thinking, "Oh my God, this is turning into a freak show!"

The medium said, "Trust me, it's not a demon. If it were I would have to bring fourteen people over, and I would have to ground you so that the demon wouldn't take your spirit over."

I hadn't slept in how many days and she's talking about demons and grounding me! All I wanted was my house back. Everything was normal until I brought those two things in.

The medium said, "I can't tell you what it is. I can only tell you that he's not there. If you want me to come back this week, I will."

Of course, I said, "Yes." But for whatever reason she never made it back over.

As the weeks passed, the noises were getting worse. One night at about 3:00 AM, I heard the noises coming from the Keeping Room. One of my golden retrievers suddenly turned into a vicious rottweiler, foaming at the mouth, snapping, growling and staring at something at the bottom of the stairs.

On Labor Day weekend my neighbor invited me over to a party. She thought it would help get my mind off of what was happening. I agreed, but asked her not to say anything about the noises *to anyone. I really didn't want people to know. While I was at the party somebody started talking about ghosts, and sure enough my neighbor tells everyone about what's been going on at my house. Of course, they all thought it was really funny and I said, "If you think it's so funny, why don't some of you come over, and you can hear these noises for yourselves?"*

Well, my neighbors came over that night along with some other people, and they all piled into my bedroom. Everyone was still pretty amused about the whole thing until the sound of fireworks in the distance began. Then the popping sound in the wall started about fifteen minutes later. "Bang! Bang!" Just like someone was throwing something up against the wall. They were all convinced it must be squirrels or some type of animal. We grabbed flashlights and proceeded up to the attic and then down to the basement, but no one could find anything. Soon, it's four o'clock in the morning and the noises are really getting intense, and no one thinks it's funny anymore. Everyone just wanted to leave.

After they left, the noises were the most intense I had ever heard. It was almost like we had really provoked whatever this was. My bed was shaking so much that I fled my room and went into the guest bedroom. It was extremely hot that night with no wind. The window behind the bed was open. I crawled into bed and as I'm pulling the sheet up, I saw one of the curtains rise up 90 degrees into the air and fall back. As I'm lying there, I felt a cold, wet mist go up my arm, shoulders and around my neck. I thought to myself, "O.K., this is different."

That night despite everything that was going on, I was so exhausted that I managed to fall asleep.

That morning I was downstairs in the bathroom drying my hair when I saw this gray, cloud-like form come from out of the corner and shoot across the room directly at my head, to the point where I had to duck. I had one of my dogs beside me. I thought, "That's it, I'm getting rid of the box and the doll once and for all!" I started to walk through the Keeping Room, but my dog refused to walk through. He started whimpering and digging his heels into the floor.

I ended up having to drag him through the room and thought, "Whatever is here is starting to become more and more comfortable."

Usually around eight o'clock in the morning the noises stop, but that morning I heard a loud crashing noise, almost like the clock had fallen off of the wall. I took the doll and box over to my neighbor's house. That night was the first night I got a good night's sleep. I didn't hear one sound. My neighbor had them for a week, and she said nothing unusual happened. I ended up taking the doll back to my friend's antique shop. She even said she would take the box as well.

The Bible box eventually ended up in a home in Rhode Island built in the 1600s. The woman who owns it said she absolutely loves it. I'm not certain whatever happened to the doll.

After the doll and the box left my house, only two other incidences occurred. I got rid of the two items on Labor Day weekend. My husband returned from sea in mid-October. He had been away while this whole thing happened. The first incident happened one night while I had fallen asleep on my stomach while watching television. I remember waking up as if I had been shaken. I looked over, but my husband was sound asleep. It felt like a steel grip around my neck. In fact it was so strong, it didn't feel human. If I live to be 100, I will never forget what it felt like!

The last incident occurred in the month of February. I remember while downstairs in my house, I heard voices coming from my bedroom upstairs, and I knew the radio and the TV weren't on. It sounded like three people were talking in mumbled voices. My husband had been down in the cellar, and as soon as I called his name, the voices stopped. That was the last thing that ever happened; but I have to tell you, if I hear a noise in the middle of the night, my heart still races.

Ghost at the Edge

OCEAN EDGE RESORT

Could such a luxurious property as Ocean Edge really harbor a ghost? According to the staff, absolutely. Ocean Edge is not a bed and breakfast, inn or hotel. It is a magnificent, sprawling self-contained resort in Brewster. Guests will find almost every amenity imaginable here, from 11 tennis courts to six swimming pools, as well as an 18-hole PGA championship golf course. Boredom is not an option here. After a long day, luxurious sleeping quarters with breathtaking views of the bay or lush gardens await the weary traveler. And if you're looking for just a little more ... Oh, I don't know ... maybe paranormal activity, Ocean Edge has a bit of that as well. What more could you ask for?

When you enter the property you will immediately notice two gargantuan houses. The first one is known as the Carriage House; the second, reminiscent of an English country manor, is called the Mansion. Both have ghostly activity, although the Carriage House seems to be the focal point. But before we delve any further, it is worthwhile to explore the property's extensive history.

Listed in the National Register of Historic Places, Ocean Edge was once the Nickerson Estate. Samuel Mayo Nickerson was the direct descendant of William Nickerson. William sailed from England to America and settled in Yarmouth in 1637; eventually he purchased an area of land known as Manomoit (the present location of Chatham) from the Native Americans.

In 1847, Samuel Nickerson left the Cape and moved to Chicago. He entered the distillery business and married a Brewster native named Matilda Crosby. Together they had one child named Roland. Samuel became an influential businessman, and served as the President of the First National Bank of Chicago in 1863. In 1890 the Nickersons constructed a large Victorian-style home back on Cape Cod. This house was known as Fieldstone Hall. They also constructed a carriage house and a windmill and kept a private game reserve on the property.

In 1886, Roland married Addie Daniels of Brewster. They had three children, Samuel, Roland Jr., and Helen. Tragically, in 1906 Fieldstone Hall burned to the ground; and Roland, who was ill at the time, died just two weeks later.

In 1907 Addie began rebuilding the mansion, but the architecture was altered from Victorian to something that presently resembles an English country manor, with an additional blend of Renaissance Revival and Gothic motifs. In 1942 it was purchased by the Lasalette Fathers and became a monastery. It was next purchased by the firm of Corcoran, Mullins & Jennison in 1980 and converted into the Ocean Edge resort.

It would certainly seem plausible that someone who had once lived on this glorious estate would have had a difficult time moving on. The spirit that dwells here has never been named or identified but is believed to be female. Whoever this entity is, her ghostly image has appeared to some people, but only in the Carriage House. For instance, one gentleman who was vacuuming a section of the house that was originally the barn claims to have seen the transparent image of a woman from the waist up. He described her as being matronly, with her hair pulled back and dressed in 19th century attire.

Apparently, this ghostly matron can be a bit mischievous at times. One of her favorite pastimes seems to be wreaking havoc upon people using the elevator in the Carriage House. Deliverymen have reported being trapped inside this elevator, its doors frantically opening and closing at will. This has happened so many times that some of these same men refuse to deliver goods to the Carriage House altogether.

Another strange occurrence involved a large brass chandelier. One night when the moon was full, a large chandelier that had been hanging above the stairwell in the house for years suddenly dropped from the ceiling and crashed down the staircase. Fortunately, no one was underneath.

In the mansion next door, unexplainable happenings have taken place as well. Lamps and glasses have mysteriously been known to slide off tables. Windows have been found wide open in the dead of winter, and strange noises have been heard emanating from empty rooms. On more than one occasion a pastry chef baking in the kitchen reportedly felt as if he were being embraced by a woman. One chef told of being overwhelmed by a pungent smell of lavender perfume, the kind an older woman might wear. He said the perfume was far stronger than any of the items being baked.

A medium was once invited to Ocean Edge to try to provide some information about who was haunting the property. The medium said that she had made contact with the spirits of a woman and her two servants in the Carriage House. She claimed that these entities reside in the Carriage House, where they are happy and do not wish to leave.

Could this be the ghost of Addie Nickerson? If so, why has her spirit remained? Perhaps, there may be a very simple explanation.

Spend a little time at Ocean Edge and then try to convince *your* spirit it's time to leave.

OCEAN EDGE RESORT
BREWSTER, MASSACHUSETTS
508-896-9000

Remember Me Ring

THE BRAMBLE INN & RESTAURANT

O ne warm spring evening, I traveled to Brewster for an interview with Ruth Manchester at the Bramble Inn & Restaurant. The inn includes two different historic buildings. The main building was built in 1861 and is home to the inn's critically acclaimed restaurant. In addition, there are three lovely guestrooms located on the second floor. The 1849 house, just a short stroll from the main inn, boasts another five rooms.

When I first arrived, Ruth and I sat in one of her elegant dining rooms, where we discussed some of her more unusual and fascinating ghostly tales. Ruth's stories contained material not only on the Bramble Inn, but also on another inn formerly owned by the Manchesters, known as the Pepper House. In addition, I have also included a story on a house Ruth lived in before she and her husband Cliff bought the Bramble Inn.

Ruth and Cliff first purchased a house in Brewster in 1980. It was a relatively new home, but she was informed that the house was thought to rest on an ancient burial ground.

Immediately after the Manchesters moved in, Ruth noticed the master bedroom always seemed a bit cooler than the rest of the house and had a strange odor. Her cats had the run of the house but never entered the master bedroom. After spending four happy years in the house with their three young daughters, the Manchesters began negotiations to buy the Bramble Inn. The house was then put up for sale in October of 1984 and sold the following April. Papers were passed on the Bramble Inn and the Manchesters departed their home and moved into the inn.

It was during the time when they had put their house up for sale that an unbelievable turn of events began to take place. One night Ruth remembers walking up to her bedroom, getting into bed with her husband and hearing a dog bark. Suddenly, Ruth and Cliff were surrounded by ghostly apparitions hovering over their bed. She said they appeared to be misty human figures of men and women dressed in Puritan-type clothing. This was not a one-time event. These apparitions appeared nightly until the house was sold. At times they were so shaken by these ghosts, they tried sleeping with the lights on. However, this did not seem to work, as the misty figures kept reappearing night after night. Ruth said, "We never felt threatened by them. I guess it was a feeling of sadness, maybe because we were moving to another house and they were going to miss us." I asked Ruth if she could remember exactly what the apparitions looked like. She replied, "My husband and I distinctly remember one of them. It was a man who had a pointed beard and wore a curved metal helmet, like Ponce de Leon."

After the Manchesters moved into the Bramble Inn, they never saw the ghosts again. But not long after, another presence was felt in a guestroom in the 1849 house. Ruth said, "I used to get a creepy feeling sometimes when I entered the room." Apparently, she was not alone. Over the years, several guests have reported feeling a presence in this little room, and to this day chambermaids are terrified to clean it.

Back in 1987 the Manchesters purchased another inn in Brewster called the Pepper House, a beautiful Federal Style Colonial built by Captain Bangs Pepper in 1793. They owned the Pepper House until 1996 when it was sold to another couple.

Before the Manchesters purchased the Pepper House, it had been an antique shop for 30 years. After extensive restoration, they converted the house into a delightful bed and breakfast. It sits almost directly across the street from the Bramble Inn on Route 6A.

For a time, the Manchesters relocated from the Bramble and took up residence in the Pepper House. One night a couple checked in. They stayed in Room 5, directly across from the room where Ruth resided. The next morning the couple came out of their room frantic. They said they heard horrific pounding on their door, as if someone were trying to enter. The couple said they started screaming at whatever it was to go away. The pounding persisted through the night. They became so terrified they actually moved a large highboy in front of the door. When they finished telling Ruth the story they quickly checked out, saying the inn was too haunted for them to stay any longer.

The Manchesters were shocked. They heard absolutely nothing, not a sound all night.

Another incident that took place in Room 5 happened to a couple on their honeymoon. After they had checked in, the couple claimed to have felt a presence in their room. The husband stated, "Whatever it was, I had never felt anything like it. It just didn't seem to want me there. It was really making me nervous."

Early on Ruth told a story that I thought I would save until the very end. After they bought the Pepper House, as I mentioned, it needed major restorations. One day Cliff was pulling out an old kitchen sink. Under the sink were old decrepit floorboards that needed to be replaced. As he started to pull up the old boards, he noticed something silvery and blue. It was an old ring. Now remember in the beginning of the story how I told you Ruth's original house was going to tie in? Well, I wasn't bluffing. When the two of them examined the ring closely, their mouths dropped. There was a figure etched into the blue stone. It was the man with the pointed beard and the curved helmet who had hovered over their bed for so many months. To this day Ruth still wears the ghostly ring. Mysteriously, it fits perfectly.

THE BRAMBLE INN & RESTAURANT
BREWSTER, MASSACHUSETTS
508-896-7644

A Woman in the Doorway

In the words of an anonymous woman from Brewster:

My house is a Georgian Victorian, probably dating back to the 1840s. I have searched and searched and have come up with some information about its history. The names and dates of the whole Arthur family who once lived here are all available on the tombstones in the cemetery on Lower County Road. All of the children died before their parents.

William A. Arthur was born in Brewster in 1822. He went to sea early as a sailor on ships in the foreign trade and served as a master's mate in the Navy during the Civil War. After the war, he was master of the ship 'The Kentuckian' and made several voyages in the Atlantic trade. On October 23, 1847, William Arthur and Miss Mercy C. Myrick filed an intention of marriage and were married on November 11, 1847.

I must say, there is something about this house that seems to endear the place to its former owners. Since we have moved in here, we have been visited by every living previous owner, all of whom have expressed the wish to live here again. We have owned the house for 23 years and have always assumed that the ghost that resides here is Mercy Myrick Arthur.

I went to a psychic not that long ago, and she told me that my house used to be a funeral parlor. I knew it had not been a funeral parlor because I have done quite a bit of research and know all of the families that have owned the house. The psychic went on to say that there were dead bodies all over the place. I said, "Well, thanks so much for telling me that!" She said that all of the dead bodies were in the front room of my house. I guess that must have been where they laid the children's bodies out for wakes.

In our house, you can stand in the kitchen and see directly through the next room into the front parlor because the doorways align. In this front room there is a doorway into the hallway, and this is where I would frequently see a woman walking. She would walk out of the front room and into the hallway, and always in the same direction. She was always dressed in a tight-fitting top and a long dark skirt. We were never frightened or threatened by her. I feel the ghost is Mercy, probably checking up on her children, but it's been a while since we have seen her.

We recently had a small but strange happening, and I have no idea if there is any significance or spookiness to it. One day in December I came home from a morning walk and found a bowl upside down in the middle of the kitchen floor. It was four and a half feet from the kitchen counter, I measured. Even a gust of wind from the kitchen door or a vibration from a truck would not have caused the bowl to fall. We have no pets or other possible explanation.

Another strange occurrence that used to happen involved wine-glasses. For some reason they would constantly shatter or just fall apart.

"It's Not the Dead That Will Get You. It's the Living You Have to Watch Out For."

THE BARLEY NECK INN

When owner Joe Lewis arrived, I had a hunch it was going to be great fun exploring the Barley Neck Inn and listening to all the interesting stories that accompanied it.

The structure was built in 1848 by Isaac and Mary Doane. It started out as a two-room, two-story Greek Revival. After losing her husband, Mary Doane sold the house to Captain Joseph Taylor in 1866. He added more additions over the years, greatly expanding the structure. Captain Taylor, a native Cape Codder, set a record for traveling across the Atlantic in a clipper ship from New York to Liverpool in 13 days, one hour and 25 minutes.

When Captain Taylor died in 1906, the home was sold to the Gundry family and later to Arthur and Dorina Nicoli, who were the first to turn the home into an inn. They added motel units in 1965 and turned the original part of the inn into a gourmet restaurant. Unfortunately, by 1990 the place had fallen on hard times. It was eventually sold at auction to the current owners, Joe and Kathy Lewis, in 1994.

When the Lewis' first bought the property, it was in desperate need of restoration. One day Joe's carpenter was tearing out a wall. During the process Joe heard the carpenter yelling for him. He ran over and looked inside the wall. Standing there upright was a fully made bed. Joe said jokingly, "I think the carpenter was looking for human bones. Fortunately, none were found."

Shortly after Joe and Kathy started their renovations they began conducting interviews for wait-staff positions. Some of the waitresses interviewed had worked for the previous owners and informed Joe that the inn had a ghost. He was a bit skeptical and took these stories with a grain of salt. During the renovations and the interviewing process, the Lewis' lived alone in the inn for nine months. During this time, Joe and Kathy began believing the waitresses might have been right. Doors and windows that had been closed would mysteriously be found opened. Lights that had been turned off would be found turned back on.

Joe had converted one of the rooms upstairs into an office. One day he was sitting in it with the door closed when, without warning, the door flew open, accompanied by a cold draft. At that moment Joe began to feel as though he were no longer alone. He began to smell a sweet fragrance, as if a woman wearing perfume were standing beside him. Joe said, "I know someone was there, and I think it was probably a woman." Joe said he was a little shaken by the experience. He remembers calling his mother and telling her about the ordeal. She simply replied, "It's not the dead that will get you. It's the living you have to watch out for."

Before concluding my visit at the Barley Neck, I had a hunch and asked Joe if anything unusual has ever happened to the waitresses. He paused and said, "I remember being warned from more than one waitress about how the ghost would flip the dinner trays out of their hands, sending them crashing to the floor." Apparently, this was not an uncommon occurrence. So, if you happen to be having dinner in the Barley Neck Inn's main dining room, you will never see a dinner tray being carried by the wait-staff. Now you know why.

THE BARLEY NECK INN
EAST ORLEANS, MASSACHUSETTS
800-281-7505
508-255-0212

Gangsters & Ghosts

ORLEANS INN & RESTAURANT

When Ed Maas purchased the Orleans Inn in the summer of 1996, saying he had his work cut out for him would most definitely have been an understatement.

The house was originally built in 1875 by Aaron Snow II for his wife and seven children. He was a direct descendant of Constance Hopkins, who was the first person to spot Cape Cod from the Mayflower as it sailed near Eastham in 1620.

The home first became an inn and restaurant back in the 1940s. Apparently over the years it had many different owners and at one point was even controlled by gangsters - the Irish Mafia, to be exact. The inn actually has a secret office built into the wall where hoards of cash used to be hidden.

Over time the inn fell into terrible disrepair. The building had become so dilapidated that parts of it were considered unsafe. That's when Ed Maas and his son Ryan came to the rescue. They purchased the inn from the bank in 1996 and started what turned out to be a massive restoration project, pouring two million dollars into the structure and furnishings. The inn had a grand opening in May of 1997, and Ed credits his son Ryan for overseeing the project.

Have I mentioned any ghosts yet? Well, follow me as we climb to the top of the inn, up to the cupola. Be careful not to bang your head, as the staircases get narrower and steeper. Well, we finally made it! Take a look at that exposed wooden beam. That's where Fred the bartender hanged himself in the 1950s.

Next, I'll take you to a little storage closet down below, where Paul the dishwasher hanged himself. And right outside the inn, two prostitutes were murdered in the 1940s. It's no wonder the Orleans Inn has a reputation for being haunted!

Hannah and Fred are thought to be the two ghosts responsible for some of the bizarre incidents that have transpired in the inn over the years. Unsure of the identities of the murdered prostitutes, the Maases named the female ghost Hannah. Fred, you recall, was the bartender who hanged himself in the cupola. Hannah apparently loves to play with doors. Ed explained that during restorations the two front doors were always closed and triple-bolted at night. Every morning the Maases would arrive and to their astonishment would find the two doors wide open. The doors on the second floor would also be found open after they had been locked.

During construction, one of the workers laying flooring kept hearing a cat. Ed assured him there were no cats around. The same worker also mentioned seeing a strange shadow in one of the closets, and at that very moment the door in the closet slammed shut.

About a week after the inn had its opening, Ed was visited by a bartender who had worked there in years past. She had mentioned to Ed that she had never seen the upper levels of the inn during her employment. At the time, these levels had been in complete disrepair and closed off. It was about midnight when Ed took the former bartender for a little tour. While walking down a hallway they both suddenly froze. The air in one particular spot became so cold the hair on both their necks stood straight up. They could sense they most certainly were not alone, and began to feel an eerie presence.

On another occasion, Ed heard heavy, mysterious footsteps when he was positive the place was vacant. Erin, his seventeen-year-old daughter, recently heard the faint sound of people talking. She, too, was alone at the time.

Ed remembers hearing crazy stories from former waitresses who had been employed by the inn years before. Occasionally, late at night in the dining room when the last guest had departed, the waitresses would blow out the candles on each table. As soon as they left the dining room to grab their purses, they would return and to their amazement find the candles relit and burning brightly on every table.

Another former waitress once told Ed that something had happened to her years ago that she will never forget. One night after the bar had closed she was gathering her belongings and getting ready to lock up. She was alone at the time. As she was leaving, she playfully said, "Goodnight, Fred" referring to Fred the ghost. At that very moment, out of the darkness, a voice said, "Gooodnnnnight!"

ORLEANS INN & RESTAURANT
ORLEANS, MASSACHUSETTS
508-255-2222

Something Evil in Chatham

In the words of an anonymous woman from Chatham:

My mom and I owned a real estate office in Chatham. One year we were asked to rent a particular house out for the summer. The man who owned the house lived far away on an island. I don't know if it was St. Martin or somewhere else. He asked if I would hire someone to go in and clean the house. I did the cleaning for our office at the time, so I told him that I would be happy to do it. He told me that he would even provide the linens for the tenants.

We ended up renting the house out to an older woman, her gentleman friend and her little dog. About two weeks before they were going to move in, I went over to clean the house. As I walked through the kitchen, which opened up into the living room and dining area, I put my vacuum down and all of a sudden this thing flew past my head and landed on the other side of the kitchen. When I looked down I saw a large sterling silver coffeepot. I walked over to it, picked it up and noticed the lid was bent back to the handle so that I couldn't even push it back. I turned around, and realized that this pot had come from the top of a hutch behind me.

I tried to figure out what had happened and noticed there was a large lip on top of the hutch, probably about two inches high. I stood there pondering how this thing could have flown off the hutch and land on the other side of the kitchen. I soon came to the realization that it hadn't just fallen off; it had been thrown at me. I wasn't sure what to do. I didn't want to think there was any kind of presence in the house. I just was sort of stunned. Anyway, I decided to start my cleaning and that was the only incident that happened that day.

The next day I went back and started on the living room. I knew the owner had said he would provide the linens, and he asked me to launder the sheets on the king-sized bed that was downstairs. When I walked into the bedroom I noticed there were footprints on the bed. I pulled the cover back and discovered the sheets on the bed had blood on them. The blood wasn't dark; it was bright red. I thought maybe the caretaker had been in, but I really didn't know what to think. I stripped the sheets, took them over to the laundromat and continued with my cleaning.

In the house there were quite a few antique tables and on every table in every room were little ceramic antique pillboxes with loose lids. After polishing a table, I would walk into another room to continue polishing. Upon returning, I would find the little pillboxes on the floor with the lids securely on.

I got the sheets from the laundromat and put them back on the bed. The next day, I noticed that the bed had been walked on again, and when I pulled the covers back there was blood on the sheets again, too. That's when I decided to call my mother. I knew I had to get this house ready for the tenants that were coming, and I was becoming really scared about being in this house alone. I also noticed that the pillboxes were doing the same thing again.

When I walked upstairs, I noticed there was a picture of the owner hanging on the wall. When I returned on the third day, the picture of the owner was now face down on the floor. It had a glass picture frame and I thought it was odd that the glass wasn't broken. I picked it up and hung it back on the wall.

The fourth day, my mom received a call in the middle of the night by the police, saying that the back door of the house was wide open. When we walked in the next morning, we realized the door could not have been opened from the outside because it had been bolted shut from the inside. It could only have been opened from the inside. At that point, I had my mom stay with me while I finished the cleaning.

On the last day I was there, I went upstairs to finish cleaning and found the picture of the owner face-down on the floor again. I picked it up and hung it back on the wall.

The woman checked in on Saturday. My mom and I decided that we weren't going to say anything to her about what was going on. We didn't want to worry her. The woman came into our office on Monday, and I still can remember her standing there with a long white envelope. She said, "I just need to talk about some problems that we're having in the house." My mom and I just looked at each other. The woman said, "I thought you were going to provide clean linens."

I said, "What do you mean?"

She said, "Well, the linens were all bloody."

Now I knew that I had already washed them twice. Then she mentioned that she and her boyfriend would be sitting in the living room, and they would hear someone upstairs walking back and forth for hours. Her little dog was racing back and forth and was absolutely terrified. She said to me, "Do you know if there are any ghosts in the house?"

I said, "I don't know anything about that." I can't remember if she checked out of the house early, but we never heard from her again.

When the owner came back at the end of the season, he called us and we went over to see him. He said the house was immaculate and he was very pleased. About a week or so later the caretaker was summoned to the house, because the owner wanted to talk with him about winterizing the place. When the caretaker arrived, he discovered the owner was dead. He had shot himself in the head.

The Ghost of Abigail, a Sea Captain's Wife

Not more than a stone's throw from the bustling shops of Main Street in Chatham, rests a sprawling, 19th century weathered and shingled Cape that was once owned by a lovely Chatham native. She would prefer to remain anonymous, so I will refer to as Emily.

Emily's house is filled with memories of joy, romance and tragedy. It is a house like many others on Cape Cod, a house deeply tied up with the past. Let's listen to Emily as she takes us back in time to the previous century, when the house was occupied by a young sea captain named Steven and his beautiful wife Abigail, and later shares her own experiences there:

From what the records show, Abigail married Steven when she was approximately 16 years of age. Steven was probably around 20 and had just recently acquired his captain's license. They were both from the Chatham village area and probably grew up together. The first year they were married, Steven had a wonderful opportunity to captain a ship and sail across the world, bartering and trading as he went. I believe he was headed for China or somewhere in that region.

The voyage, if everything went as planned, would probably have taken about a year. Abigail decided to stay home and wait for his return. She was with child, but had the help of her relatives to assist her. During the first year, she gave birth to a baby boy, but Steven did not return at the end of the year. Abigail received word from other sea captains who had sailed in the same region that Steven was doing well. Abigail assumed everything was fine.

After the second year her child became ill. It was thought that she blamed herself for not doing something right and would frequently stand in the yard atop the bluff looking out to sea, feeling that something was wrong. People began to tell her that Steven was probably lost at sea and that she needed to put it behind her and move on with life. She refused to listen and kept a lantern in the upstairs bedroom, hoping the light would guide him towards the house.

Abigail began to withdraw from her family. She wasn't eating; and since Steven had been gone for two years, there was virtually no money. Her mother thought it would be best if she let a friend of Steven's, who was very fond of Abigail, take care of her. She refused and continued to withdraw. Finally, her family began to pull back and in that third year, her child died.

She eventually was forced to rent out the rooms in the house to people that would help with the upkeep. However, she refused to move out of the room that was hers and Steven's. In fact, she became very angry when someone wanted it. Abigail would sit for hours in that room, looking out to sea, hoping to spot his ship. She would even set a place setting for him at the table each night.

That spring there was a horrific ice storm. Abigail, who was becoming ill probably due to stress, did not stoke the fireplaces properly the night of the storm. The house turned bitterly cold, and she was found dead the next morning.

The following October, Steven returned home, only to find the house dark and closed down. The people that had rented the rooms left after Abigail died. Apparently Steven was shipwrecked and at one point held captive by pirates.

The townspeople told him about Abigail's death and where she was buried. When he went to the cemetery and walked up to her gravesite, he said, "Why couldn't you have waited for me?"

Sometimes when I have had a traumatic experience, such as a loss in the family, I have come back up to the house, and on more than one occasion I have seen Abigail standing in the yard, atop the bluff, looking out to sea. She is a very pretty woman with chestnut-colored hair, and she always wears a cape which blows in the wind. She's not transparent; she's as solid-looking as you or I. Strangely, I have only seen her in the fog. The feeling I get with her is one of great emptiness and that she wants to be where Steven is, but she can't seem to reach that far.

I always tell this to people: Homes belong to the people that have lived in them, and if there's a tragedy, the house absorbs some of it. I don't care what anyone says, it's got to.

Trapped in Time

The ghost of Abigail described in the previous story is not the only Chatham spirit Emily has encountered. On the town's famous Shore Road, just off Main Street, rests another haunted house with which she is familiar:

I will take you back to May of 1993. A friend called me and asked if I wouldn't mind cleaning her house and getting it ready for renters. Her mother had passed away the year before, and she couldn't decide if she was going to live in Maryland or come back and live in the old homestead in Chatham. I told her I'd do the best I could.

She said to me, "Just remember, there's something wrong with the house." She was referring to her standard poodle that would sit at the bottom of the stairs and growl and whimper, refusing to go up. I told her it was probably because her mother had just passed away and the dog might still smell her clothes or something. She said, "No, it's something else and if you go there, don't be frightened by it."

I said, "Don't worry, it's not going to frighten me."

So I went into the house and began to clean. The next-to-last day I was there, I started to hang white lace curtains. About five minutes after I finished hanging them, I saw that the curtains had been pulled off of their hooks and were lying on the floor. I called my friend that night and told her that something was going on in her house. She said, "I told you, if you're frightened don't go back in there." But I insisted that I wanted to get to the bottom of it.

This is something that still frightens me to death when I talk about it. The following day, the realtor came over and said the house looked perfect. I said, "Fine," and thought I'd just send my friend the bill and that would be that. But after the realtor left, I walked up the old steep staircase to the second floor. When you reach the top of the stairs there is a landing. On the top of the landing, there is a small bedroom to the right and a large bedroom to the left. Directly in front is the attic, which is open with a large window from the ceiling to the floor.

As soon I reached the top of the stairs I felt a cold draft. I thought that perhaps the realtor had left a window open, and for some reason something drew me into the small bedroom on the right. I went into the room and sat down on the bed. Well, that's when it started to happen. All of a sudden, I began to hear voices downstairs. I heard this woman's voice say, "No, you can't go upstairs. She's upstairs. You're not going upstairs."

I then heard, three men's voices say, "We have come to take her home."

The woman replied, "No, you're not taking her. She's upstairs and she's going to stay upstairs."

I thought to myself, "O.K., just be quiet." Something told me to get off the bed and walk up to the window, which faces out to sea. I stood at the window and suddenly a girl appeared in the room with me. She was probably 18 or 19 years of age, with tears running down her face. She was very homely looking, but had a determined face. She had some kind of old-fashioned bag with an oriental design on it. I assume her clothes must have been inside. I could sense what was happening. Evidently, she must have come to this house for help from Mrs. Batchelder. The Batchelders lived in the house back in the 1800s. I believe that the voices from downstairs were those of her relatives who were trying to stop her from running away.

The voices didn't stop. I could still hear them coming from downstairs. I knew that she was trapped, and I felt trapped because she was standing beside me. I could feel her touching me in a way that said, "Can you help me?" Suddenly, I turned and looked towards the attic and coming out of the attic window was a striking man wearing a blue sailor's uniform, beckoning the woman to come with him. Through the window I could even see the old Packard ship he had sailed in on, docked in the water. Apparently, she was going to run off with him, and the captain on the ship would marry them.

In my mind I could hear her communicating with me. I believe she wanted me to stand guard while she crossed over into another world with him. Evidently, he was where he was supposed to be, but she was still trapped in that room. I have never sensed such a strong emotion of anguish. It scared the living day lights out of me! I felt I was being drained of my being in order for her to move through whatever she had to, to get to that other point. I began to get the feeling that if she couldn't be with him, she'd rather take her own life, and I wonder if she did commit suicide. Maybe that's what had been trapped in that room for all those years. It was the first time I felt as if the death of a person were pulling me into some type of vortex that I couldn't escape from.

The woman walked out of the bedroom and into the attic. She then joined the sailor and together they turned into a blurred outline and disappeared. Just before she left, she turned to me with a look of elation on her face. She was almost glowing.

I must have sat there for an hour; I was just so drained. I had never experienced anything like it before.

Maria Hallet & Black Bellamy

S amuel Bellamy, or Black Bellamy as he was called due to his jet-black hair and swarthy skin, was one of the most infamous and successful pirates of his time. He was born in England and as a young man had managed to make his way across the ocean to Cape Cod in search of relatives.

During his brief time on the Cape, Bellamy met a young woman named Maria Hallet, and the two instantly fell in love. He told Maria about his plan to sail south and salvage the treasure of the Spanish Fleet that had recently sunk off the coast of Florida in 1715. It was documented to that over 2000 chests of newly minted coins were aboard. He made a promise to her that he would return with the mighty treasure and they would marry.

But Sam needed a financial backer. He befriended a Newport goldsmith named Paul Graves Williams, and together they sailed down the East Coast with the dream of recovering the treasure. Neither Bellamy nor Williams had any idea they'd have such competition once they reached the approximate site of the wreck. Divers were sent by the King of Spain and sailed from other parts of the world to salvage the treasure. The two men and their crew, running low on supplies, decided to give up. Far too embarrassed to return to New England empty-handed, the men decided there was another way to obtain wealth. They quickly made the transition from treasure hunters to pirates.

In 1716 they joined forces with a more experienced pirate named Benjamin Horngold. It was said that Horngold had just finished training a man who would go on to become one of the most notorious pirates the world has ever known, Edward Teach, better known as "Black Beard." Over time the crew voted Captain Horngold out, and Bellamy became the new Captain.

During Bellamy's absence, Maria was said to have given birth to a boy with black hair. When she had become pregnant she moved to a secluded spot in order to conceal her pregnancy, as townspeople of that era had no tolerance for unwed mothers. However, the child's life was not long. Maria hid the baby in a barn, and he supposedly choked to death on a piece of straw. When the authorities found the child's body, Maria was imprisoned for neglect. She somehow managed to escape from her small jail, and was therefore accused of being a witch, although it was believed that the prison guards took pity on her and left the door to her cell unlocked.

Meanwhile, Bellamy and his crew, now sailing a ship they had captured in the Caribbean called the *Whydah*, were headed back up the coast toward New England. Supposedly, he was returning to be united with Maria.

The year was now 1717 and Bellamy had reached Wellfleet when a horrific spring Nor'easter took him and his crew by surprise. The *Whydah* capsized and only two crew members survived. Maria Hallet and Samuel Bellamy would never see each other again.

It turns out that the story of Black Bellamy and the *Whydah* is far more than a mere legend. In fact, treasure hunter Barry Clifford successfully found the remains of the *Whydah* off the coast of Wellfleet near Marconi Beach in 1984. This was the first excavation of a pirate ship in world history, and Clifford found a fortune in gold bullion. Today, the "Expedition *Whydah* Sea Lab & Learning Center," located at the end of MacMillan pier in Provincetown, is a great place to learn more about this historic discovery.

What remains less conclusive is the legend of Maria, whose ghost many say still haunts the dunes of Wellfleet. Eyewitnesses have seen the ghostly apparition of a woman walking the cliffs and peering out at sea for a lover who would never return.

The Deacon

Long ago, there lived a man known as Deacon Collins, who was an active member of the First Meeting House in Truro. This house of worship sat atop a hill known by many as the "Hill of Storms." The Deacon never joined his family during worship, but would always sit on the Deacon's Bench at the foot of the pulpit so he could keep his eyes on the members of the parish who were sleeping.

The Hill of Storms was a tough climb for anyone, and as the Deacon grew older he found it increasingly difficult to make the journey to the Sabbath meeting. To make the trek easier he purchased an old gray horse, and on the first Sunday of every month, Communion Sunday, he fastened a jug of sacramental wine to the saddle.

Watching the old Deacon ride his horse up the hill was said to be a comical sight, particularly on Communion Sunday. Apparently the Deacon became obsessed with fears that the sacramental wine would not be delivered on time and would whip his horse in an attempt to make it trot faster than it was able. Congregation members would often remark how it appeared as if the poor old horse were coming apart: The front half looked like it was going in an easterly direction, the back half in a westerly direction.

On one particular Sunday in the spring, tragedy struck. As usual, the Deacon began his wild ride on the old horse up the Hill of Storms, past the many people who were walking to church. Suddenly, the hoof of his horse struck a young boy, a boy the Deacon was quite found of. He saw the child fall to the ground, but was so obsessed with delivering the wine that he kept on riding. The horse, however, was so startled by the collision that it reared off course, stumbling over tombstones in a nearby graveyard. The Deacon managed to get the horse back on the path and delivered the wine to the front door. Sadly, the young boy who was struck by the horse died.

A service was held for the boy the next day, and when it came time for the minister to hold up the jug of sacramental wine, the Deacon walked over to the child's body and then departed the meeting house. It is said that he mounted his horse and slowly ambled away, never to take part in a service again.

Upon the Deacon's death, his body was buried in a nearby graveyard on the Hill of Storms. Townspeople claimed that the hoof marks left by the Deacon's horse after it had trampled over the graves never disappeared until his death.

Some say at midnight, if the moon is full, on the first Sunday of the month, the Deacon can sometimes be seen or heard riding his old horse through the graveyard with his jug of wine splashing beside him. When he finds an ancient tombstone, the Deacon climbs down from the horse, kneels and prays. He then mounts the horse and together they drift back to another time.

The Dead Poets Guesthouse

CARPE DIEM GUESTHOUSE

And nothing can we call our own but death,
And that small model of the barren earth
Which serves as paste and cover to our bones.
For God's sake, let us sit upon the ground,
And tell sad stories of the death of Kings –
How some have been deposed, some slain in war,
Some haunted by the ghosts they have deposed...

– William Shakespeare, *Richard II*

On a quiet street in Provincetown, just steps away from the hustle and bustle of the center of town, stands an impeccably restored 19th century guesthouse known as the Carpe Diem. Each room is dedicated to a renowned literary figure. But what really gives the Carpe Diem its soul are its two owners, Rainer Horn and Jurgen Herzog. Originally from Cologne, Germany they moved to Provincetown, purchased the bed and breakfast, and opened for business on Valentine's weekend 1999.

When I conducted the interview for this book, they appeared to be in the beginning stages of uncovering the inn's history. For example, they discovered the house was once a funeral home. The other fascinating secret is that, you guessed it, the Carpe Diem guesthouse is haunted.

Rainer informed me that the first weekend the guesthouse opened for business there were numerous disasters. While he and a number of guests were sitting around the breakfast table with a fire crackling in the background, he remembered hearing a strange noise. Rainer turned around and saw water pouring down the front door. A pipe had begun to leak from the bathroom above. Soon after, someone broke a window. The two owners had absolutely no idea how to fix a window, and Jurgen said in a panic, " Rainer, what should we do?" Rainer replied, "We're going to have to find window nails or something." Jurgen went down to the basement and found himself staring at a bag marked "window nails" that was sitting in the middle of what had always been an empty countertop. Rainer believes something, or someone, was trying to test them in the beginning.

As time went on, stranger events began to transpire. One former owner and manager talked about a haunted room, which at the time was Room 9 and is now named the William Shakespeare Room. One housekeeper said that when he enters this particular room, he often senses a presence and feels that someone is watching him or standing behind him.

The basement seems to be another place of heightened activity. This same housekeeper mentioned that while in the basement he once heard someone talking in his ear and could actually feel someone's breath on the back of his neck. But when he turned around he could find no one.

Another housekeeper who once lived in the basement reported seeing the mysterious shadow of a human figure walking into his room. Even Rainer has felt a presence in two different areas of the basement.

The Eugene O'Neill Room located on the first floor seems to drive the present manager a little crazy. Many a time after the room has been cleaned and locked, he has walked back into the room and found the bathroom sink dirty, as if someone has just been shaving. He has also found the imprint of a body on the bed.

Guests are not immune to having paranormal experiences, either. Rainer remembers two very spiritual women, both therapists, who stayed in the William Shakespeare Room. The next morning Rainer asked one of the women how she had slept. She replied, "Well, it was kind of weird. I remember a voice telling me to 'Get up and get out!'"

Another guest entered the guesthouse and immediately announced that there was a spirit in the house. After sleeping in the William Shakespeare Room, she was confirmed in her opinion, having heard strange noises and seen eerie shadows throughout the night.

One guest who stayed in the Tennessee Williams Suite mentioned that the door opened by itself four times in the middle of the night, even after it had been locked. This guest told Rainer he had to put the suitcase against the door to keep it from opening.

Rainer also told me about a woman who suddenly sprang out of the guesthouse hot tub (which is located next to the basement), got out of the water, came to him and asked, "Who was that dressed in those weird clothes walking into the basement?"

"What do you mean?" said Rainer who was thoroughly confused.

The woman replied, "Well, while I was sitting in the hot tub, I saw a man and a woman dressed in clothing that dated back well over a hundred years. I saw them walk right into the basement. I've seen a lot of weird clothes in Provincetown, but I've never seen anyone dressed like that!" No one was ever found.

Paranormal activity seems to fluctuate at the Carpe Diem. At times the guesthouse will become extremely active, and then for reasons unknown things will quiet down.

One of the ghosts is believed to be a former manager named Kevin who died years ago. Apparently he loved the inn so much his spirit is thought to have remained, looking after things. The identities of the other ghosts remain uncertain. Only one thing is for sure at Carpe Diem: Guests are encouraged to "seize the day" ... for who knows what nightfall will bring!

CARPE DIEM GUESTHOUSE

PROVINCETOWN, MASSACHUSETTS

508-487-4242

800-487-0132

Fade Away

THE MARTIN HOUSE RESTAURANT

The Martin House is one of the finest dining establishments in Provincetown, serving such delicacies as grilled rack of wild boar, slow-roasted rabbit legs, and "drunken" roasted half-duckling. It's no wonder food critics can't stay away from this place. The restaurant has received rave reviews from the *Boston Globe, Boston Magazine, Cape Cod Life,* and *The New York Times* to name but a few.

The restaurant's cozy and romantic 18th century atmosphere is unforgettable. The Martin House is a classic three-quarter Cape overlooking majestic Provincetown Harbor and is believed to have been built in 1755. By the mid 19th century its owners were actively involved in the abolition movement. The house is one of three documented safe houses in the town, used to harbor slaves who were escaping to freedom in Canada. The house harbors two hidden rooms; the first is referred to as "snug harbor," formed by the massive chimney complex of the house. The other room, referred to as the "secret room," is a third-floor loft. It is accessed by a small narrow staircase.

By the early 1900s the house was purchased by the Hatch family and operated as a boarding house for the elderly. During the 1960s the house came under the ownership of a woman named Mrs. Lovely and apparently fell into disrepair by 1978. However, the house was rescued by Eileen and Romaine Roland who transformed it into an elegant French bistro. In 1991 it was purchased by the Martin family.

The place is just chock-full of ghost stories. Glen Martin believes that the ghosts that inhabit the Martin House come from this century as well as past centuries. His sister and a few other people have played witness to an apparition of a man who has appeared in 19th century garb in one of the second-floor dining rooms. Glen's sister described this presence as resembling someone she had once seen in a 19th century portrait. The first time she laid eyes on this ghost, she became so frightened that she actually jumped down an entire flight of stairs from the second floor without injury.

On occasion Glen and his father have also seen someone out of the corner of their eyes in the same room. But whenever they turn to get a good look, there is nothing. In the other dining room adjacent to this room, guests have reported seeing shadows and hearing peculiar noises.

The small dining room on the first floor is no stranger to ghostly activity, either. One woman told Glen that when she was a very young girl she remembered seeing a small man in that room while she was eating with her family. Now much older, the woman claims to see a type of convoluted mass of energy or ectoplasm. She believes this mass of energy is made up of different people who once lived in the house. The small man she first saw is thought to be one of the former owners, Mr. Hatch.

Glen had a chance to speak with a woman (since passed away) whose aunt used to live in the boarding house during the 1930s. She frequently visited her aunt and took notice of Mr. Hatch's peculiar habits. The woman said he used to save everything, particularly paper. Apparently Mr. Hatch was obsessed with saving paper, thinking that it may come in handy some day. Glen recalls something incredibly strange that happened when they first purchased the building. Very often when someone would walk into the bathroom they would find paper towels or toilet paper folded into tiny perfect squares. At first Glen thought it was a practical joke, but no one claimed to know who was responsible. This went on for three years, and Glen eventually found out that Mr. Hatch used to save paper napkins by folding them into small perfect squares, just like the ones they kept finding.

Another bizarre incident happened to a woman who used to prepare breakfast at the restaurant. She claims to have seen the outline of men pacing back and forth in front of the bathroom. Originally, the bathroom used to be the Birthing Room just off the kitchen, and it makes sense that men would have been frantically pacing back and forth there, waiting for their wives to give birth. Glen and his father have also witnessed this phenomenon first-hand. Just opposite the bathroom is a fireplace with a large painting over the mantle. Glen has seen shadows of men pacing back and forth in the reflection of the glass frame of the painting as well.

On the second floor there is a passage to the "secret room." At night, employees are afraid to enter this room, as some have felt as if they have been touched by a person while inside the room. The room also experiences extreme temperature changes, so much so that hard liquor is one of the few items that can be stored there.

The most astounding sighting at the Martin House occurred in September of 1991. The Martins had purchased the property the previous May from people Glen had known fairly well, as he had been employed at the restaurant waiting tables when he was in college. On a September evening Glen remembers working alone in the kitchen washing pots and pans. Suddenly he felt something and quickly turned around. He found himself staring at John, one of the former owners, who was smiling at him.

"Hey John, what are you doing here?" said Glen. At that point John began to slowly disappear, to fade away starting from the legs up until the only thing that remained was his head floating in mid-air ... and then he vanished altogether! Glen was in a state of disbelief and quite shaken by the incident. Shortly thereafter, Glen received word that John had passed away that very same day.

THE MARTIN HOUSE RESTAURANT
PROVINCETOWN, MASSACHUSETTS
508-487-1327

BIBLIOGRAPHY

Cape Cod Life, "The Legend of Hannah Screecham." Introduction by Greg O'Brien, Story by Edward Cabot Storrow, Jr. October 1999, pages 119–127.

Clifford, Barry. *The Pirate Prince.* New York, New York: Simon & Schuster, 1993.

Coogan, Jim, & Sheedy, Jack. *Cape Cod Companion.* East Dennis, Mass.: Harvest Home Books, 1999.

Gamble, Adam. Editor. *The 1880 Atlas of Barnstable County.* Yarmouth Port, Mass.: On Cape Publications, 1998.

Reynard, Elizabeth. *The Narrow Land.* Chatham, Mass.: Chatham Historical Society, 1978.

Other Books from On Cape Publications

Haunted Inns of New England by Mark Jasper $14.95

Howie Schneider Unshucked: A Cartoon Collection about the Cape, the Country and Life Itself by Howie Schneider $11.95

Baseball by the Beach: A History of America's National Pastime on Cape Cod by Christopher Price $14.95

In the Footsteps of Thoreau: 25 Historic & Nature Walks on Cape Cod by Adam Gamble $14.95

Cape Cod by Henry David Thoreau (Audio) performed by Casey Clark $19.95

1880 Atlas of Barnstable County: Cape Cod's Earliest Atlas Edited by Adam Gamble $39.95

Walking the Shores of Cape Cod by Elliott Carr $14.95

Cape Cod, Martha's Vineyard & Nantucket the Geologic Story by Robert N. Oldale $14.95

Cape Cod Light: The Lighthouse at Dangerfield by Paul Giambarba $9.95

Sea Stories of Cape Cod and the Islands by Admont G. Clark $39.95

Coloring Cape Cod, Martha's Vineyard & Nantucket by James Owens $5.95

Quabbin: A History & Explorer's Guide by Michael Tougias $18.95

Until I have No Country: A Novel of the King's Phillip War by Michael Tougias $14.95

New England Wild Places: Journeys Through the Back Country by Michael Tougias $12.95

~ Available Wherever Great Books Are Sold! ~

www.oncapepublications.com